We would like to thank our

Interior graphic designer and illustrator
David Basye (www.dbasyedesign.com)

Writing Coach
Marcy Pusey

Editors
Ida Basye
Melodie Bogantz
Katrina Burton
Alina Hare

How to Visit 47 U.S. National Parks
in 2 Months on a Budget

THE ULTIMATE ROAD TRIP GUIDE

CHRISTINA BOGANTZ AND MELISSA RIOS

TABLE OF CONTENTS

INTRODUCTION

from Melissa's perspective

We are two cousins, Christina and Melissa, who decided to go on a crazy road trip. We spent two months in the spring of 2017 living out of a pickup truck. During this time, we drove around the United States visiting all the mainland national parks (forty-seven at the time). When we were planning our trip, we lacked guidance in many areas and had to learn along the way. We wrote this book as a travel guide that we wish we had had when considering, planning, and executing our road trip. We want to show you how possible a big road trip like this is.

It was not a simple decision. We had reasons not to go, worries about our safety, concerns about our friendship, and apprehension about missing out on events back home. But, in the end, we were so glad we went, and we were able to work through everything.

This trip is simpler than you might think. We want to share with you how to best prepare. We have guidance on how to plan your route, how to plan for the parks, how to build the platform of the truck to sleep on, and how to organize the truck. We will suggest what to bring along and what to leave behind, and things you should discuss with your travel buddy before you go.

We also want to share with you our best "on the road" tips. These include our best food ideas, recipes for cooking on the road, and safety tips. We tell you about our discoveries of the best and worst places to spend the night. We share tips on finding water, showers, and laundry facilities, and we even give entertainment ideas for long drives. We will break down the entire cost of our trip to show you how we did it for under $3,000 each.

Not only did we make amazing memories on this trip, but this trip also changed our lives. We returned home with more confidence—more reason to believe we could do hard things that we set our minds to. We became more open to adventure and more willing to try new things. This trip pushed us out of our comfort zone and made us more responsible. We did more than we thought we ever could, and our friendship grew because of it all.

We hope that because of this book, you will find the same things. We hope you find an eagerness to dream, confidence to follow through, and the means to do it all. Then you too can embark on an ultimate road trip.

CHAPTER 1

A CRAZY IDEA

from Christina's perspective

With college under our belts, we each found ourselves full time jobs and went to work. We weren't seeking adventure at the time, but adventure found us when my sister-in-law Ashley told me about a crazy road trip. Her idea for an ultimate road trip was to visit all the United States mainland national parks in two months. This idea definitely piqued my interest. But it seemed to me like something other people would do, and I thought it was insane for someone like me. My mind started wandering and I couldn't help but share the idea with my cousin Melissa. Our initial thoughts and conversation went like this:

C: *Okay, this idea is crazy! But it does sound really cool and I bet Melissa will agree.*

C: **"Want to go to all the United States national parks on the mainland with me? We can drive it and hike and have so much fun."**

M: *I chuckled at Christina's message and decided to just go along with it for the moment. "Yeah right!" I thought, but I quickly replied:*

M: **"Ha! Yes, I do! But how and when?"**

C: *"Wait! She is actually considering this? I was not expecting her to be on board. Am I on board? This is crazy! This isn't practical, is it? Well, let's take the idea and run with it."*

C: **"This Spring?"**

M: *"Wow is she serious?"*

M: **"How long do you think it would take?"**

C: *"There's no way this is going to happen, but it's fun to think about. I mean, can I just up and leave my job for a trip like this?*

C: **"Just over two months."**

M: *Ha! No, there's no way this would really happen. Well, I'll just see what she is thinking.*

M: **"But, what do we do about our jobs?"**

C: *Wait a second...we are actually considering this insane trip?*

C: **Are you seriously considering this trip...like is it even possible?**

Melissa and I both thought that visiting the forty-seven national parks sounded like an incredible trip. But neither one of us got our hopes up too much because it didn't seem realistic. We had all the reasons in the world not to do a road trip. We were both just out of college. Spending so much money on a trip like this and not working for such a long time didn't seem like a wise decision.

But from the first thought of this road trip, neither one of us could shake the idea. Ashley had lit a fire in us, and Melissa and I now had a burning desire for adventure. We couldn't help but think about how much fun it would be living a new, crazy, different lifestyle of adventure on the road. We kept thinking about all the memories that we would make together and the opportunity to become even better, closer friends. We couldn't help but imagine all the amazing places that we would see. And we were excited for the potential of becoming closer with our Creator by seeing so much of His handiwork.

We kept talking about the trip and dreaming about it. The more we talked about the road trip, the more excited we got! Eventually we started asking each other if this trip could be a reality. And so we began looking into whether or not it was possible.

CHAPTER 2

IS IT POSSIBLE?

from Christina's perspective

W e loved the idea, and it was all we could think about. It consumed us. Deep down we both wanted to do the road trip. So first we needed to see if it was possible. Being 100% open and honest with each other, we discussed things like - Would we have the time for it? Would we have the proper vehicle and housing for it? And could we afford it?

Did We Have the Time?

The trip was suggested to us as one long road trip, but we also explored the possibility of doing the trip in two sections. We considered visiting half of the parks in one year and the other half another year. This idea simplified some aspects of the trip. Splitting the trip into two road trips would have made the trip look less daunting than one massive road trip. Planning one trip now and one trip later sounded easier. Doing two trips would be nice so that we could spend less money all at once. That way we would also have more time to make money for part two.

But dividing the trip in two parts would have made the route complicated for us Ohioans because the majority of the parks are out west. We also were concerned about leaving our jobs twice within two years. That would frustrate our employers. The idea of splitting it up into two trips also left us with the fear of getting too caught up in life and not going back to finish part two. After weighing the pros and cons, we decided that if we were going to do the trip that we would do it all at once. Go big or go home!

We knew from the beginning of planning this trip that the longest we wanted to be gone was two months. We are both home bodies, and we weren't sure if we could manage being away for any longer than two months. We had loved ones that we were going to miss and who were going to miss us. And we couldn't afford to be traveling for more than two months. We had to go back to work.

We both looked to our parents for guidance on whether or not it was a good use of our time. Our parents were very supportive of the idea, and they believed that it was a good opportunity for us. My dad thought that if we didn't take advantage of our "freedom" and do the road trip while we could, that we might regret it. He encouraged us to take advantage of the opportunity.

My family and Melissa's family 100% backed us up and they were excited by the idea of the road trip. I'm sure they thought that we were a little crazy. But they were very supportive. The support from our families really helped Melissa and me feel confident that the trip was a good idea. It was crazy, but a good kind of crazy. We were young and had no huge responsibilities, and we were ready for some adventure.

We knew that branching out on our own would be a good experience for both of us. Having always lived at home, we thought that the time on the road would be great for personal growth. We knew we would miss our friends and family and the comforts of home, but it would be good for us to live and learn on our own.

We knew we would get homesick and lonely, but we were excited for the opportunity. We knew that everyone was just a phone call away and that we would only be away for two months. Both of us were especially excited for the opportunity to see God's creation. We believed that a trip like this would be healthy for our relationships with Him.

Would We Have the Proper Vehicle and Housing?

If we were going to do the road trip, what kind of vehicle is necessary? We would need something reliable and big enough for us to comfortably live out of for two months. Melissa had recently purchased a 2014 Toyota RAV4™ SUV. It seemed like a potential vehicle for an adventurous trip around the United States. It was spacious enough for both of us and for all the stuff we would need to pack. The gas mileage on a vehicle like this was very appealing. But traveling in Melissa's SUV would require us to set up camp at a campground every night.

The more we were thinking through the road trip the more we realized how nice it would be to be able to sleep in the vehicle that we chose for the trip. Being able to sleep in the vehicle would give us so much more flexibility. It also would save us the time and hassle of setting up tents and taking tents back down. Not to mention it would also save us so much time in the planning department. Planning out campsites for two months would be hard. But sleeping in the vehicle opens up another whole world of options!

Our other option for a vehicle was my family's 2006 Chevy Colorado™ pickup truck. It doesn't get the greatest gas mileage, at an average of 20 miles to the gallon, but it was a pretty reliable vehicle. I thought it might work for the trip so I asked my parents if they would be willing to let Melissa and me rent their truck from them for two months.

They were a little reluctant at first, seeing as the truck was used quite frequently around the family farm. But they said we would be able to work something out. I started researching how to make the bed of a pickup truck livable. It looked like the Chevy Colorado truck would be the vehicle for us and our home!

Can We Afford This?

We both had some money saved up, but could we actually "spare" it? We needed to be responsible with our money and think about the future. We didn't want to spend the money on the road trip and find ourselves regretting it down the road (pun intended). We both took a good hard look at our bank accounts. We discussed how much we would need to set aside or earn so that we could make the road trip a reality.

Assuming we were taking the Chevy Colorado truck, sleeping in it, cooking our own meals, and driving at least 16,000 miles we did some rough estimates. We came up with the estimate of $7,000 total. Split evenly our estimated expense was $3,500 per person. Between the money in our account and the time we had to make up the difference, it looked like it was financially possible for us. (See chapter 5 for a deeper look at our budget.)

We wanted to do it! Finally, we were both 100% committed to doing The Ultimate Road Trip! We felt like this trip was a once-in-a-lifetime opportunity, and we were beyond excited for what lay ahead. By this point it was January. In less than four months after the suggestion from my sister-in-law we were going to do it!

Chapter 2 Takeaways:

Consider whether or not you have the...
- ❑ Time to spare
- ❑ Proper vehicle
- ❑ Adequate housing
- ❑ Financing

～❀ CHAPTER 3 ❀～

PLANNING

from Christina's perspective

I t was early 2017 when we began planning the road trip! And we were realizing that two months is not a very long time to make it around the United States and stop at forty-seven national parks. We had a lot of details to figure out so that we could make the road trip a success.

After doing some research, we discovered that as far as we could tell no one had done a trip like this. So we would have no recommendations on our route and no help deciding how much time to spend at each park. Melissa and I were starting from scratch. We didn't even know if it could be done. But we were going to find out!

At first, all the stuff that we needed to plan seemed overwhelming. What time of year can we make this work? How do we pick a good route? How do we plan how much time to permit for each park? And is two months actually enough time to complete a trip of such proportion? And each of these questions led to many more questions. We couldn't plan one aspect of the trip, like planning what time of year to go, and then move on to the next aspect, because each was dependent on the other. And so the research began!

What Time of Year?

The first big question that set the ball rolling was, what time of year can we make this work? This led us to try and figure out when it would be best to leave our jobs and when is the best time to visit each park. Melissa's job was relatively flexible. As a data analyst it wouldn't matter what time of year she left. But for me, I didn't want to leave my work at the farm during peak season, which is July through October.

We also didn't want to do the trip over the summer when the parks are heavily visited. And we didn't want to do the trip too early where we would be visiting the northwestern parks while they were still buried in snow. Summer, fall, and winter were out of the question for us, so sometime in the spring was our best option.

So, we started looking for the best two-month window in spring. We found a list of all the mainland national parks and we began researching what we could do at the parks between the months of March and June. We found that anytime in spring looked good for the eastern, southern, and western parks. The weather would be nice for hiking and for sleeping in the truck. And the majority of these parks shouldn't be overly crowded.

But we also found that even in June our options of hikes were limited in the pacific northwest due to the heavy snowfall. It looked like late spring would give us the best opportunity but even then, we knew our hiking options would still be limited. Because of the heavy snowfall up north, we decided to visit the southern parks before heading up north. This also left us with a rough idea of what our route would look like.

Next, we started looking at the calendar and we tried to pick out a two-month window for the trip. We were looking at the time frame of March, April, May, and June and the biggest holiday in that time frame was Easter. Easter was on April 16th in 2017 so why not leave the day after Easter? If we managed to see all the parks within the two-month time frame then we would be home by mid-June! So, just like that, we had a date picked! April 17th, 2017 was going to be the day we embarked on The Ultimate Road Trip!

In hindsight, how did we like the time of year we went on the trip? Because of the time of the year, we understood that some parks were going to be covered in snow and we were going to have limited hiking options. We loved the hikes that we were able to do, and we were still very happy with our timing. Overall, it was comfortable truck camping weather. Both summer and winter would have been miserable for truck camping.

One thing that we hadn't considered regarding the weather was the amount of fog that we would encounter. In the Smokies, Bryce Canyon, Olympic, and in several other parks, we encountered heavy fog. It slowed us down slightly, but we managed to stay on schedule. Even though it decreased our visibility and lengthened our drive time, we thought that the fog was pretty, and it gave us the opportunity for more unique photos.

The Route

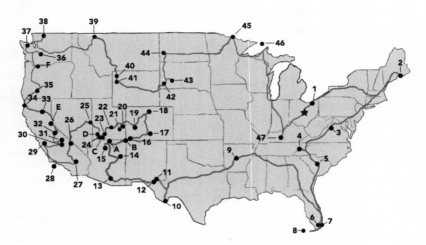

1) Cuyahoga Valley National Park, Ohio
2) Acadia National Park, Maine
3) Shenandoah National Park, Virginia
4) Great Smoky Mountains National Park, Tennessee/North Carolina
5) Congaree National Park, South Carolina
6) Everglades National Park, Florida
7) Biscayne National Park, Florida
8) Dry Tortugas National Park, Florida
9) Hot Springs National Park, Arkansas
10) Big Bend National Park, Texas
11) Carlsbad Caverns National Park, New Mexico
12) Guadalupe Mountains National Park, Texas
13) Saguaro National Park, Arizona
14) Petrified Forest National Park, Arizona
15) Grand Canyon National Park, Arizona
A) Horseshoe Bend, Arizona
B) Four Corners Monument, Colorado/Utah/Arizona/New Mexico
16) Mesa Verde National Park, Colorado
17) Great Sand Dunes National Park, Colorado
18) Rocky Mountains National Park , Colorado
19) Black Canyon of the Gunnison National Park , Colorado
20) Arches National Park, Utah
21) Canyonlands National Park, Utah
22) Capitol Reef National Park, Utah
23) Bryce Canyon National Park, Utah
C) Peekaboo Canyon, Utah
D) Kanarra Creek, Utah

24) Zion National Park, Utah
25) Great Basin National Park, Nevada
26) Death Valley National Park, California/Nevada
27) Joshua Tree National Park, California
28) Channel Islands National Park, California
29) Pinnacles National Park, California
30) Sequoia National Park, California
31) Kings Canyon National Park, California
32) Yosemite National Park, California
E) Lake Tahoe, California
33) Lassen Volcanic National Park, California
34) Redwood National Park Trail, California
35) Crater Lake National Park, Oregon
F) Multnomah Falls, Oregon
36) Mount Rainier National Park, Washington
37) Olympic National Park, Washington
38) North Cascades National Park, Washington
39) Glacier National Park, Montana
40) Yellowstone National Park, Wyoming/Montana/Idaho
41) Grand Teton National Park, Wyoming
42) Wind Cave National Park, South Dakota
43) Badlands National Park, South Dakota
44) Theodore Roosevelt National Park, North Dakota
45) Voyageurs National Park, Minnesota
46) Isle Royale National Park, Michigan
47) Mammoth Cave National Park, Kentucky

A rough idea of our route fell into place due to the weather and climate of the different parks. Because we are from the great Midwestern state of Ohio, we decided to visit the eastern parks first and then work our way around the United States in a clock-wise route.

Next, we needed to map out our route. I am the kind of person that likes to have a hard copy of things instead of using the online version. I like to be able to hold on to the paper and feel the pages. So naturally I went and picked up a copy of every single inland state map and several United States maps. I left the store with what felt like twenty pounds of paper maps.

Some of these maps turned out to be helpful, especially the maps of the entire United States. Sometimes we didn't have cell service on the road, and we had to go with the old-fashioned technology and use a paper map to get to where we needed to be. But to find the best possible route, the newer technology turned out to be way more helpful than my twenty pounds of paper maps. I found some maps online that marked every national park and I started using the Google Maps™ service to find the fastest route from park to park. As I was putting the route together, I was constantly running things past Melissa and making sure we were on the same page.

★ **Relationship Tip:** *Keeping your travel buddy in the loop for any decision will help ensure that you start your trip off right.*

While researching the parks in more depth, we realized that there were several national parks on islands. Before we started planning the trip, we had no idea that there were any national parks on islands. Now we were looking at at least three, all of which we would need to take a ferry to go see them.

We also found out that seeing Mammoth Cave National Park during early spring would be an issue. Because of the snow melt and rising water levels in the cave, we would have to skip this park and do it later. What we had thought would be the easiest part to plan turned out to be not as straightforward as we originally thought. This brought to our attention the need to research each park before settling on a definite route.

We decided to continue creating a potential route and we would later go through and research each park in more depth. We wanted to pick the most efficient route and then come back later and make sure we could see the places that we wanted to see at the time that we would be there. We also added a few "bonus stops" to our itinerary. These were stops that we would like to visit even though they were not national parks. We had to keep these bonus stops to a minimum, but there were a few places that we really wanted to see like Horseshoe Bend, Kanarra Creek, and Lake Tahoe.

There are very few parks in the Midwest and on the East Coast, so that part of our route was pretty easy. But the route was not quite so obvious once we were looking at the multitude of parks out West. While planning our route for the parks in Arizona, Utah, and Colorado, I started plugging national park visitor centers into the Google Maps™ mapping service and then mixing up the order of the national parks until I found the quickest, simplest route for us. It took a while to type in all of the parks and to figure out a good route, but doing this on a computer was so much easier than using paper maps. (How did people travel before technology?)

While I was constructing the route, I put all the national parks on a park "hit list" in the order that we planned to visit them! Then we counted them to make sure I didn't miss any. Ah, Oh! I only had forty-six national parks on the list. It turns out that I had accidentally missed Capitol Reef National Park in Utah! Thankfully this was still very early on in our planning and it didn't drastically change the original route. How awful it would have been to go all over the country and come home just to realize we skipped a park! Melissa thought my mistake was funny and she didn't lose faith in our route. But I'm pretty sure this led us to both double check, or even triple check, that we had all the parks on our "hit list."

★ ***Relationship Tip:*** *Be aware that your travel buddy is only human and that they are bound to make mistakes.*

Looking back on the trip, our route served us very well. We made it to all the parks and six non-national park stops all within our two-month timeframe. I call that a success! We had a few non-national park stops that we would have liked to have visited but we didn't have the time for them. These were places like, Canyon De Chelly, Mount Hood, and Sleeping Bear Dunes. But we have no regrets! Keeping the road trip to two months was important to us, so we had to sacrifice a few destinations. We can go back to destinations like these another time!

The Itinerary

Next, we wanted to research each park and get an idea of what we wanted to do there. The discovery of Mammoth Cave National Park not being open for cave tours in early spring made us want to dig into every park a bit deeper, so we wouldn't run into any similar issues while on the road. While investigating each park we also listed possible hikes, overlooks, and scenic drives that sparked our interest. We used resources like TripAdvisor, national park apps, and the book *National Geographic - Guide to National Parks of the United States* (Schermeister - National Geographic - 2016).

We also asked friends who have visited various national parks for their input on what we wouldn't want to miss. We tried to research everything that each park had to offer. In doing so, we were able to get a rough idea of how much time we wanted to spend at each park. This was hard. We wanted to see it all, but we had to limit ourselves because of the time frame in which we wanted to complete this road trip.

We wrote down how much time we wanted to spend at each park. Then, we wrote in the driving time that it would take us to get from one park to another. This began to evolve into a rough day-by-day itinerary for the trip. Our original itinerary was a couple weeks longer than we wanted it to be.

So we went back through our itinerary and made our driving days a bit longer to cover more ground in a day. We also trimmed off time at some parks to keep the two-month time frame a reality. We decided to only briefly visit the parks that were close to home because we could easily come back to them another time. This opened up more time for the parks that were further away from us, like Yosemite.

We also tried to leave some flexibility in our itinerary in case we had a problem with our vehicle or one of us wasn't feeling well. So every two weeks we would make sure we had a day that wasn't packed full with things to do. We also left a half day open for an oil change at our halfway mark.

To keep the trip to two months long we both had to be willing to drive a long distance in a day. We agreed that we would drive all day long, from time to time, if that's what it took. Sometimes that meant driving up to twelve hours in a day. But having long driving days is what gave us more time to go hiking.

We could have taken a couple days to drive across Texas. But because we drove all the way across Texas in one day, we were able to do a long hike up to Guadalupe Peak. Yes, the drive across Texas was kind of boring and it would have been nice to split the drive into two days. But it was worth it to keep on driving so that we could hike more and see more sights inside the parks.

We never lacked the motivation to drive. We had ways of making the drives entertaining (see chapter 12), and the ever-changing scenery kept the drives fun. The main thing that kept us motivated to drive was the excitement of what lay ahead. We were always excited to be making our way to our next destination. We were fueled by the desire to see the national parks. After seeing one national park we thought, "Let's go see the next one! And the next one! And the next one after that!" It was like an addiction. We had to see more parks!

The parks were the biggest motivation that got us through some long days of driving. But coffee and good snacks played their part as well. Caffeine and sugar are quite the combo and will make the drive more pleasant. On the longer drives we enjoyed a little more coffee than usual to give us an extra boost of energy.

And at the very beginning of our road trip we decided to "reward" ourselves for every state border that we crossed. We both have a love for all things caramel. So every time we crossed a state border we enjoyed a piece of caramel candy. It was fun to have a little treat, recognize our progress, and celebrate the little victory. We had to improvise for our drive across Texas though. We were a little discouraged not to be crossing state borders for the entire day.

★ *Relationship Tip: Celebrate the little victories together!*

We each had different strengths and weaknesses when it came to driving. And we learned to use them to our advantage. I am from the country and am not very good at driving in heavy traffic. Melissa is from the city and is very comfortable with driving in traffic. So when we found ourselves in Los Angeles at rush hour, Melissa took the wheel. On the other hand, I am more alert than Melissa at night, so I took more of the late-night driving shifts. We could rely on each other to help us in the areas that we were lacking. This definitely helped us cover more ground in a day.

★ *Relationship Tip: Know each other's strengths and weaknesses and adjust accordingly. Your weakness may be the other's strength.*

Looking back, we were very happy with our itinerary and our experience in each of the parks. We got to explore the parks and get a taste of what they have to offer. There are some parks that we definitely want to go back to and explore more. I mean, there will never be enough time to see everything in every park. But we are so happy for what we did get to see!

We are beyond grateful to report that we never had any major problems with our vehicle and neither one of us got sick. So the extra time that we had allotted for events like those allowed us to shorten some long driving days, stay longer at some coffee shops to post blogs, and give us extra time to hike. Also, having the extra time available in case we needed it was a huge stress reducer.

Chapter 3 Takeaways:

Considerations for what time of year to do your trip:
- ❑ Is the weather going to be ok for truck camping?
- ❑ How long can your trip be?
- ❑ Does the timing of your trip affect your job?
- ❑ Are there big events that you can't miss?

Considerations for your route:
- ❑ Efficiency
- ❑ Road conditions
- ❑ Double check that you haven't skipped a destination

Considerations for your itinerary:
- ❑ The weather in each park and its effect on hiking options
- ❑ Allow for extra time at stops that excite you
- ❑ Allow some flexibility for vehicle issues and health issues
- ❑ Allow time for vehicle maintenance and repairs

TRAVELING TOGETHER

from Christina's perspective

T he most common question that we got about the road trip was in regards to our relationship. Before the trip, the question was, "Are you going to hate each other by the end of the trip?" During the trip we got, "Are you still getting along with each other?" And after the trip we heard, "How are you two still friends?" We managed to live together in a tiny space for two months and remain friends. Not only did we remain friends, but we became better friends. Before the trip we made sure we would be each other's ideal travel buddy by discussing our interests and expectations for the trip. And during the trip we tried to always be open and honest with each other—which helped us get along.

Find Your Ideal Travel Buddy

Some people might enjoy doing a road trip alone. That was not the case for us. From the beginning, we knew that if we were going to do this trip, we wanted to do it together and not alone. In our minds, half of the adventure is the experience we would get to share together. Doing a trip all over the country by ourselves sounded too lonely and boring. We were a perfect match for each other because we shared the same interests and expectations for the road trip.

★ **Relationship Tip:** *Before the trip, make sure you and your travel buddy share the same interests and expectations for your road trip.*

We both knew we wanted to travel inexpensively, even if that meant roughing it for a bit. But we also wouldn't want to be so frugal that we wouldn't enjoy ourselves. The idea of saving money by camping or sleeping in our vehicle appealed to us more than spending money to stay in hotels. The idea of saving money by cooking our own meals instead of eating out was an idea that we both liked. We both enjoy cooking and are pretty good cooks, if we do say so ourselves!

But perhaps the most important preference we shared was our tastes in hikes, and they are as close to identical as can be. Together we looked into several parks. We saw each other show excitement for the same hikes and views. We knew that our hiking interests would be very close to the same. Easy hikes are always fun, but we also like strenuous hikes. Some people would look at strenuous hikes as not worth it or as torture, but we look at them as an exciting challenge. We were both in pretty good shape and health from our active lifestyles. And we were both capable of similar things. Neither one of us is an avid rock climber, snow skier, or anything like that, but we would definitely be capable of hiking all day any day.

We also made sure that our expectations lined up in regards to driving. We had a lot of driving ahead of us and we needed to be on the same page. It is very important to agree on how often you switch drivers and to agree on how much driving you will do in a day. We were both willing to drive equal amounts and we enjoyed switching drivers pretty often. Most of the time we would switch drivers at every fill up. On the longer driving days we switched at every half of a tank of gas, that way neither one of us got too burned out on driving.

Though our expectations were very similar, we knew that sometimes we would have to compromise. Whether it be how far we would drive that day, how long we would stay somewhere, what music we were going to listen to, the temperature in the truck, or whatever, we knew it would be impossible to agree on absolutely everything. From time to time we had to give and take a little.

★ **Relationship Tip:** *Be willing to compromise.*

Melissa and I had different cell phone providers and sometimes only one of us had service. So there were several times where one of us would want to stay at our source for Wi-Fi a little longer than the other. So we had to figure out a compromise. Having different cell phone providers was actually a great advantage. Usually at least one of us had cell service that way.

Looking back, the two of us were each other's ideal travel buddy. We almost always agreed on the important decisions of which hikes to do, what to eat, and where to stay for the night. And when we didn't agree, we found a way to compromise.

How Would it Affect Our Relationships?

We all know that spending twenty-four hours a day, seven days a week for two months is a long time to spend with anyone. Even if it is your best friend, you're bound to have disagreements and get on each other's nerves. So, Melissa and I wanted to make sure we would enjoy each other's company and not ruin our relationship as best friends.

Could we spend so much time together and not hate each other by the end of the trip? To us, it wasn't even a question. We were excited by the idea of hanging out together for two whole months. We knew that we would not only get along for the duration of the trip but that the trip would make us even closer friends.

Our relationships came first. It was more important to us to keep a healthy relationship than to complete the road trip. We knew that there would be some days that would be harder than others. Our friendship was going to be tested. We knew that we would not always see eye to eye on everything, but we knew we would be willing to work through any differences. That's what friends do.

We agreed to tell each other right away if something the other person was doing was annoying us. This was very important for a healthy relationship. Telling your travel buddy in a nice way that what they are doing annoys you is better than letting the issue go on for the duration of the trip unaddressed.

★ *Relationship Tip: It is better to get an issue out in the open rather than let it fester inside.*

Before leaving on the trip we also gave each other "warnings" about ourselves just to give each other a heads up. For instance, I told Melissa that I like quiet, calm mornings and that I usually wake up hungry. Just sharing simple things like this was helpful to know what to expect of each other. It set us up for success.

★ *Relationship Tip: Tell each other about your quirks, habits, and routines, so that they know what to expect.*

Because we were close friends before the trip, we already knew a lot about each other. We knew what each other liked or disliked and what made the other happy or upset. For example, I knew that Melissa really valued talking to friends on the phone. It helped to know things like this ahead of time about each other so that we could try to approach situations with these things in mind.

★ **Relationship Tip:** *Spend time with your travel buddy before the trip. Get to know your travel buddy's likes and dislikes and try to be mindful of them.*

We are both introverts, me more so than Melissa. So, on the trip we would both need some time and space to ourselves. Alone time would be hard to come by while traveling together for so long. But we agreed that we would find a way to make it work. Even if that meant hiking the same trail but not together. Finding time away from each other would be key for having a healthy relationship.

★ **Relationship Tip:** *Finding time away from each other is key for having a healthy relationship.*

We found it easiest to get alone time before bed. So that is when we would split up and give each other some space. We each would either walk around the parking lot, sit in the cab of the truck, or lay in the bed of the truck. Trying to be safe, we stayed close enough that we could see each other, but we gave each other enough privacy to make calls or do whatever we wanted to do by ourselves.

It wasn't always easy to get along. Our friendship was put to the test. About three weeks into the trip we had some struggles. Up until that day everything had been going well and we were getting along fine. But that day was hard. After getting very little sleep we woke to some cold, wet, nasty weather. We were sleep deprived, uncomfortable, and exhausted. Nothing was going as planned. The weather was not ideal for hiking. Melissa wasn't feeling well. I burnt my hand while making coffee and later I spilled my coffee in my seat. We were a mess, worn out, and not ourselves. There was definitely some tension and frustration between us. Instead of keeping our frustrations to ourselves, we opened up to each other and told each other how we felt. After we talked things over, there was really no issue and only some misunderstandings. We worked it out, shed some tears, and became closer through it.

★ *Relationship Tip: Be open with each other and share your feelings. Friendships may be strained but the best friendships are worth straining for.*

The road trip definitely strengthened our friendship. We found ourselves finishing each other's sentences and thoughts all the time. We joked about not being able to have our own thoughts because we were always having the same thoughts. We didn't even need to talk to each other because we could read each other like a book. The road trip took our friendship to another level.

Chapter 4 Takeaways:

Find your ideal travel buddy with the following considerations in mind:
- ❑ Hike expectations
- ❑ Driving interests
- ❑ Trip duration
- ❑ Trip expenses
- ❑ Your personalities
- ❑ Your physical abilities

BUDGETING AND MONEY

from Melissa's perspective

Money can be a big roadblock for any trip, but I want to show you how financially manageable a big road trip actually is. In order for it to be manageable, it is important for you and your travel buddy to be in agreement on a few things before you embark. It is also important to understand the expenses of your trip beforehand and to keep track of them as you go.

Before You Go

Choose What's Important

Decide with your travel buddy what is most valuable to you both, and what you are both willing to live without. This is essential to having a good time. If you aren't sure if your values line up, sit down with your buddy and write a list of the possible expenses. Include things such as restaurants, hotels, campgrounds, and excursions. Then, rank the list in order of importance to you both. For us, we were willing to spend more money on excursions and experiences but eating out or paying for campgrounds ranked very low.

★ *Relationship Tip: Learn what each other values most and what you can both live without.*

After you know what is important to you, save some room in the budget for some spontaneous splurges on these important things. We were only on day eight of our trip when we decided to take our first splurge. We arrived early in the morning at Biscayne National Park in Florida. After a disappointing sunrise due to fog, we meandered along a path beside the calm bay.

"Well, what else should we do?" I said. The path we took was short, and the park was ninety-five percent underwater. "Let's ask at the visitor center," we decided. But when there, our faces fell as we listened to the lady say, "the half-day sailing trip has already left." Yet, a glimmer of hope came when she said, "But you can take the full-day sailing trip. It goes out to an island where you will snorkel and paddle board—all for just $159." We shot a glance at each other, but our thoughts were abruptly interrupted with, "Oh, and it leaves in about ten minutes."

Our heads were racing, and we thought, "It's only day eight! That feels like so much money right now. But what else would we do!? It's not like we will be back any time soon." Under this time pressure, our analytical minds had to make an uncomfortably quick decision. We shot another look at each other with confidence this time. "Yes! Let's do it!" The next ten minutes were a whirlwind, but soon we were grinning as we stepped into the boat and were off.

Christina and I decided that this was an instance where we wanted to splurge to get the most out of our road trip. We would have missed all ninety-five percent of the park if we had not gone. The money spent was worth the experience.

★ *Relationship Tip: Pay attention to how the other feels about spending money on things, and don't pressure each other.*

Sometimes, though, our choices about where to spend money or not spend money were not quite as fun. This proved true on the very same evening after the sailboat adventure. We had decided to continue driving for three hours down the Florida Keys. We were heading down the beautiful Highway 1 towards our next destination, Dry Tortugas National Park.

We had an excursion booked to visit the island early the next morning. We wanted to sleep somewhere close to the ferry dock. But by the time we arrived at Key West, it was close to midnight, and we were so exhausted. We pulled into a large parking lot only to read, to our dismay, many signs threatening fines and towing that said: "No overnight parking." "Let's try some other parking lots," we said. Yet we only found more of the same. Big hotels were all around us. We were so tired. All we wanted was to sleep, but yet, we had decided on no hotels, and we had each recently spent $159.

We continued to drive around. Just when we thought we should give up, we pulled into a parking lot with a pay machine. After investigating, we learned that we could pay to park for twenty-four hours. It was exactly what we needed. It was not free, and it was noisy. But staying in a parking lot like this rather than a hotel was the type of sacrifice we had agreed upon to make our trip possible. As we closed our eyes, we only hoped to get sleep among the roosters crowing and the noisy pub life crowd nearby.

Budget

After you choose what is most important to you both, the second thing you need to discuss is your budget. You may not have the exact same budget when it comes to souvenirs or maybe even restaurants. Yet, it's still helpful to calculate it out and both have an understanding of the full costs. An estimation to use as a guideline is all you need.

Here are the main things to budget for:

1) Gas: We did some simple math to figure this out. If we took the Chevy Colorado™ truck, it would get about twenty miles per gallon. We estimated we would drive at least 16,000 miles, so that meant we would need about eight hundred gallons of gas. At an average of $2.50 per gallon at the time, we guessed we would spend at least $2,000 on gas.

2) Food: This one you have more control over depending on how much you want to eat out versus cook yourself. We estimated we would spend an average of twenty dollars per day on food for sixty days for a total of $1,200.

3) Excursions and Tolls: We under-estimated these expenses. Several parks require boat rides to explore or visit the park. Others require extra fees to enter or take tours (see chapter 9 for more details on these parks). Toll expenses also pile up quickly when driving this much. In the future, I would have budgeted at least $1,250 total for the two of us.

4) Vehicle Expenses: You will likely need two oil changes on the road. We also needed to buy a cap for the truck bed, materials for the truck platform, and pay rent for borrowing the truck from Christina's parents. Paying for a tune-up inspection prior to the trip is also wise. Your budget will greatly differ depending on what supplies you need to purchase, but our total truck expenses were close to $930.

5) Campgrounds: We estimated on the high end here. We guessed we would spend thirty nights at campgrounds for twenty dollars per night. This came to a total of $600. (Spoiler alert: we spent way less here!)

6) Camping and Cooking Gear: If you don't already have camping and cooking gear you will need to budget for

those, or consider borrowing from family and friends (see chapter 8 for all the gear you will need). You can also often find great deals on gear at thrift stores and off-price retail stores.

7) Souvenirs: This one is totally up to you. But you should know that the national park visitor centers do have some pretty good gift shops; so, keep this in mind.

Remember, if you are traveling with someone else, you get to split most of these costs in half.

In addition to these main six expenses, we considered two other things when looking at the expense of the trip.

First, we looked at the cost of living after we returned home. We thought through questions like: How long would it be until our next paycheck? Did we have enough money saved so that we didn't have to worry about any bills or payments before then?

After we chose our adventure start date, we both had to tell our employers about our trip. We were very grateful that they both allowed us to put our jobs on hold and pick them back up afterward. Having jobs to come back to was a huge relief for both of us, and made us feel at ease about leaving.

The second thing we planned for was the cost and possibility of flying home. We didn't have any expectations to need this emergency budget. But if there were a family emergency, an injury, or an illness that caused us not to be able to finish the trip, we wanted to be prepared. Having this emergency fund gave us peace of mind during our travels.

The Budget Breakdown

We want to share with you our exact breakdown of costs to help you establish your budget and set expectations. Of course, you can be more or less frugal than we were. Our trip cost in 2017 was about $2,800 each making the cost only $45.25 per day.

If this sounds too expensive to you, remember that this is a two-month-long trip, and we visited forty-seven different parks plus bonus stops. Consider how much a one- or two-week vacation would cost you. If you are like me, you'll be as frugal as possible, but still spend $2,000 to $3,000 after flying, renting a car, staying in a hotel, and eating out. And that's only for a week or two! But here, with this kind of road trip, you will spend the same amount of money, if not less, as you would on a typical vacation. Not only that, but you will get more out of it if adventure is what you are seeking.

Here are our money details. Our six biggest expenses, in order, were gas, food, excursions, truck rental and upkeep, campgrounds, and tolls. Of those, gas, truck expenses, and tolls are all fairly easy to calculate before leaving. Excursions, food, and campgrounds can be determined based on how much you are willing to splurge. We cooked much of our food ourselves and often slept in free camp areas (more on these later). These two decisions saved us hundreds of dollars. Here is our breakdown of expenses:

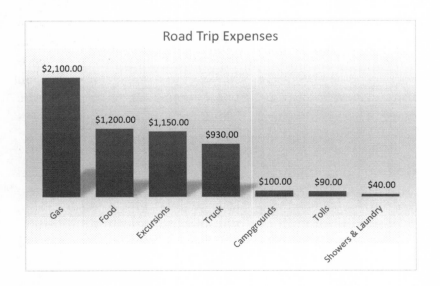

Consider a Cashback Credit Card

Another thing we discussed before the trip was how to handle shared expenses on the road. Rather than each using our own credit or debit cards and keeping track of the split, we decided to open a card in my name. We did not apply together for a joint credit card; I simply authorized Christina as a user of the card. This gave her a card with her own name. This proved valuable to us for two reasons.

First, we could get a card that met our specific needs. I chose a card that had a three percent cash back for gas and two percent cash back for groceries. Although not much return in the grand scheme of things, this did save us about $185.00. This added up to a few free tanks of gas.

The second reason for this card was that it gave us a way to easily keep track of our shared expenses. Gas, groceries, coffee breaks, and excursions all went on this card. Individual purchases like souvenirs were the only things that did not go on this card. Then, in the end, all we did was split this balance in two and each paid for half.

Please note that opening a credit card to go into debt for a trip is never a good idea. We paid off this credit card in full on every month's due date. Also, please only consider this option if you are confident in your buddy's ability to pay half of the bill. If this is a concern, you can each pay separately and split costs as you go. This will take more intentionality, but it will be worth it if this is a struggle.

★ **_Relationship Tip:_** _Be open with your travel buddy about money. If you have money concerns discuss them ahead of time._

On the Road

Keep Cash in an Envelope

We have a couple of tips for a smooth ride after you have embarked on your adventure. For starters, make sure you have cash on you. For us, tolls, campgrounds, and parking lots all required cash along the way.

To make things easy, we kept an envelope of cash in the truck while we drove. Both of us contributed even amounts of cash into the envelope as we went. We paid almost one hundred dollars in tolls along the way, so that pre-stocked envelope of cash was very handy. Some toll areas will take a picture and send a bill to the owner of your vehicle. You may want someone to check the mail for them while you are away. But if you don't, many states offer an online option to pay and you can look up and pay the amount due online.

Having money in a variety of denominations was helpful. Tens were good for campgrounds and parking expenses, and we needed ones for tolls. Quarters also were essential for laundry and showers.

Keep Track of Expenses as You Go

The last word of advice for spending money on the road is to keep track of expenses as you go. We used the Google Docs™ web-based word-processing program to give us both access to edit and enter transactions. Yes, the credit card kept track of most of our expenses, but there were a few times when that credit card was not used.

For example, we had grocery and excursion purchases prior to the trip and prior to getting the shared credit card. These went in the Google Docs program. Any cash expenses like tolls or tip money also went in the shared document. This eliminated confusion later when calculating how much we owed each other.

I should also note here that keeping receipts to record cash expenses can be helpful. Yet, after you have recorded them there is no need to keep every receipt for the rest of the trip. In fact, this can be harmful to your relationship. Especially if your buddy gets annoyed by clutter. So take it from me, and don't stuff them throughout the truck.

★ **Relationship Tip:** *Keep clutter (like old receipts) to a minimum.*

Chapter 5 Takeaways:

- ❑ A big road trip isn't as expensive as you might think.
- ❑ It's crucial to discuss with your travel buddy your choices on where you'll want to splurge and where you'll want to save.
- ❑ Create a budget plan of all the estimated costs before you go.
- ❑ Make sure you keep cash handy in the vehicle for things such as tolls, campgrounds, and parking.
- ❑ Decide if a shared credit card is a good way to easily split expenses and keep track of everything else in a shared document.

ᵆᴗ CHAPTER 6 ᶿᵆ

BUILDING OUR HOME ON WHEELS

from Christina's perspective

We definitely got a late start on building our home on wheels. So the main goals for our build were to keep things quick, cheap, and simple. And we achieved those goals. We didn't invest too much time and energy into converting the pickup truck, and it still had everything we needed. In this chapter we will look into finding a truck cap, building the platform, and adding finishing touches.

Finding a Truck Cap

A hard-shell cap is what we were looking for. We needed something that we didn't have to tear down each day, like a tent style cap. A hard-shell truck cap would keep out the weather and the sound better than a tent style cap. It would also allow us to park just about anywhere for the night. So the first step to making the bed of the pickup truck into a home was finding a good truck cap!

The cap needed to have windows with screens so that we could get some ventilation while sleeping in the back. Also, I thought it would be nice if the cap had a window that lined up with the window on the truck itself. This would allow us to reach from the cab of the truck into the bed of the truck. I looked into getting a brand-new cap for the bed of the truck but was quickly turned off by the price tag.

After a couple of weeks of looking around, I found a good deal on the Craigslist® website. The cap definitely needed a good scrub down, but it fit! It was in good condition with no visible holes or cracks in it, so it looked like it would keep out any water. Also, the screens on the windows were in good condition. I would have to replace the lock on the truck cap. The seller was not the original owner, and he did not have the key for locking the truck cap. Other than the lock, it looked like it would be ideal!

I took it home and gave it a very thorough scrub down. I used bucket after bucket of soap and bleach and got rid of the musty, mildew smell it had from sitting outside for who knows how long. While washing the cap I didn't see any leaks in the roof which was great news! I ordered some clamps for the cap and a foam sealing strip to put between the truck cap and the truck bed. We also purchased a new lock mechanism for the truck cap.

Building the Platform

Before my dad and I could put the cap back on the truck we needed to build the sleeping platform. My dad graciously told me that if I designed the platform, he would help me build it! He has all the know-how and a large workshop with all the tools we were going to need. So I began to design.

I looked on YouTube and all over the internet (Yes, technology for the win!). There were all kinds of helpful tutorials and tours of other people's builds. There were numerous tutorials of extravagant builds where people were living full time out of their truck. Their builds were extremely fancy with many compartments and pull out drawers. Melissa and I didn't want the build to take too long, we didn't need anything very fancy, and we didn't want it to be too expensive.

We needed a simple, functional platform, one that would leave us with enough head room to move around and to easily get in and out of the bed. We wanted it big enough that we wouldn't feel too claustrophobic when sleeping. And finally, we needed one that had enough storage space below it for everything that we would require for living on the road for two months. It was important to me that we built a platform that would be easy to take back out of the truck bed and put back together. We didn't want a permanent platform.

We came up with a design for the platform that would create three large storage compartments running the length of the bed. Each of these compartments would be accessible by two removable sections of the plywood platform.

At the hardware store we got some ¾ inch plywood, a few 2x4's, screws, and brackets. That was it. With my dad's help we dove right in! For an in depth look at our build, see the appendix.

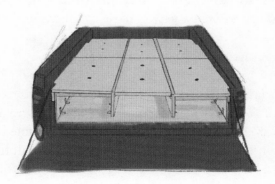

Over the course of two days our platform was complete! I was very happy with the build! On the day that it was completed, Melissa came over and inspected and admired the platform. At this point it was twenty-two days before we planned to hit the road. Having the platform completed made us both very excited! It made the trip feel that much more real to both of us. It was no longer just a dream; it was actually happening.

Several people suggested that we paint or stain the platform. Although either of these treatments would help preserve the wood if it got wet, we opted out. We would have had to take the time to disassemble the platform, paint or stain it, and reassemble it. The platform was completed just over three weeks before we left, and we didn't have the time. With no paint or stain we had more reasons to make sure the truck cap was 100% leak free!

Finishing Touches

With the platform being complete, I could put the truck cap back on! The best way to see if the truck cap leaked was to test it in the rain. With rain in the forecast, I left the truck out of the garage to see how it did. When I checked it the next morning, I was a little disappointed to see that there was a leak. So the truck moved back into the garage where we caulked around the window and tried to seal up the leaks.

★ **Relationship Tip:** *Make sure there are no leaks in your roof. A dry travel buddy is a happy travel buddy. And if your travel buddy isn't happy then you aren't happy either.*

At this point in the process, the truck was actually livable. But there were a few more homey touches that would make the truck bed more comfortable for us. Those homey touches were curtains and lights! My mom is very good at making things and loves sewing. I asked her if she would be willing to help me out by making curtains and thankfully, she said, "Yes."

I purchased a large blackout curtain and my mom took over from there. She cut them to size and hemmed around the edges. She did an excellent job, and we were so very thankful for her help. She made four curtains that were quick and easy to put up and take down. On the back side of the curtains (the side up against the window, she attached a small loop. The loop would slip on to the Command™ Hooks that we hung above the windows. We ended up using J-B Weld™ to secure the Command Hooks. (The original adhesive would not stay put when the cap heated up in the sun.) The hooks also doubled as a nice place to hang our keys.

These curtains did an excellent job blocking out the light so that we could sleep about anytime in any place. Looking back on our road trip, we really could not have done what we did without the curtains. They were amazing! Without the curtains we would not have been able to sleep in lit parking lots—which we did frequently. They also added a layer of insulation on the cold nights.

The next homey touch was completed by Melissa's and my cousin, Caleb. Caleb is a super handy and thoughtful cousin and he offered to install lighting for us. Originally, I was thinking that we could use flashlights and headlights to see around in our home on wheels. But the more Caleb told me about his vision for lighting, the more I fell in love with the idea. His idea was to install some LED lights and a battery so that we could have lights in the bed of the truck with a flip of a switch.

He put up two strips of LED lights. One strip was close to the cab of the truck so that we could see around in our home, and one was near the tailgate so that we could cook on the tailgate at any hour of the day or night. He did an excellent job and we were so thankful for his help. The lights felt like a very extravagant upgrade from the original plan of flashlights and headlights. He even loaned us all the supplies and did this work for free!

Though not much of a "build," this last homey touch made our lives so much easier. We added a paracord string around the tailgate. This made it so that we could close the tailgate with ease from inside the truck. The string around the tailgate is a must.

Below is a breakdown of our build expenses. In total we spent less than $400 on the materials for the platform.

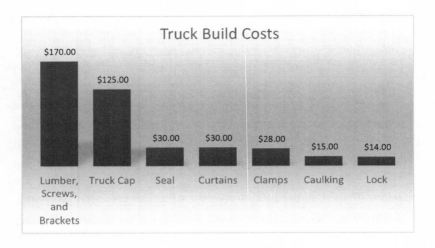

Chapter 6 Takeaways:

❑ Find friends and family who will help you!

ORGANIZING OUR HOME ON WHEELS

from Christina's perspective

We did a lot of organizing before we hit the road, but some of it did evolve while traveling. We tried our best to have a place for everything and to keep everything in its place. Our three main spaces for storage were under the platform, above the platform, and in the cab of the truck.

Under the Platform

We designed a lot of storage space below the platform, because we knew we would need a lot of supplies for two months on the road. As shown in the build of the platform, (see chapter 6) there were six boards that made up the platform. They were removable for easy access to the storage space below.

The three compartments closer to the tailgate were easily accessible. So we used them to store things that we used every day, like our kitchen supplies. These three compartments were usually accessed by opening the tailgate. We could remove a top section of the platform to access what was inside, but we found it to be just as easy to slide the items in and out from the tailgate.

Inside the compartment on the left we had a storage bin. The bin could easily slide in and out from below the compartment. We used this storage bin to help keep our larger kitchen supplies organized.

In the middle compartment we had more storage bins that helped keep everything neat and organized. This is where we stored most of the cooking and eating utensils. Also, our water jug was kept in this compartment. We had a non-skid shelf liner mat that laid underneath the water jug to keep it from sliding around. Having the water jug stored near the tailgate made it easy to access for cooking and filling our water bottles before heading off on a hike.

In the compartment on the right, we stored our stove, fuel, and shoes. Along with kitchen storage, this compartment served as an entryway closet. It was nice to be able to step onto the tailgate at night, take off your shoes, slide them into the compartment, and go to bed.

My bed was behind the driver's seat and Melissa's bed was behind the passenger's seat. So the storage section underneath each of our heads would be our main area for personal storage. We each got approximately one-sixth of the storage space under the platform. Our section for personal storage was referred to as our closet. This closet was adequate space for what we needed to pack. We both had to be very conscious of what we were packing so that we didn't overflow our closet.

★ *Relationship Tip: Use only your share of the closet space and keep it organized, so that your travel buddy doesn't have to mess with your stuff.*

Between our closets, in the middle compartment, was a bin that we called our pantry. It was where we kept the food that we didn't need to get into every day. It had packets of instant mashed potatoes, Ramen noodles, canned vegetables, canned meats, and things like that. We would get into the pantry once every three or four days and pull out what we thought we would use within the next few days. We would put these items in our more immediate use storage toward the tailgate. (See chapters 8 and 10 for our packing lists.)

Above the Platform

Some things were used so often that we chose to leave them above the platform where we could easily access them at any time. We had to decide what was important enough to leave out instead of tucked away under the platform.

The snack bin was definitely important enough to keep above the platform. It was a 1x1x1 foot storage cube that fit nicely in the space between our pillows. It had things like granola bars, trail mix, crackers, etc. Of course, we wanted our snacks accessible at all times but more importantly we needed a barrier between our pillows. After a few nights of us waking up with our heads inches away from each other, we decided we needed to do something about it, and our snack bin was a perfect barrier.

★ **Relationship Tip:** *Unless you enjoy waking up with your face inches from your travel buddies' face, put a barrier between your pillows.*

By putting this storage cube behind the cab window, we made the snacks easily accessible from the cab of the truck. It was a win-win for us! We slept better at night and could easily reach a snack while on the road. It was also in a convenient place in case we got hungry in the middle of the night. No matter what, we could quickly grab a snack.

Right next to the snack cube we kept a box. The box eventually got referred to as the nightstand. We would basically empty our pockets into it before bed. We put things like our pocketknives, lip balm, headlamps, pepper spray, phones, and wallets in there. The nightstand was always easily accessible. It also doubled as a nice extra barrier at night.

We kept the snack cube and nightstand on top of the platform day and night. Several other items we kept on the platform during the day and moved them into the cab of the truck every night, creating more room for sleeping. Most prominent of these were our bathroom bags and our lunch bin.

The bathroom bags were home to many of our daily essentials, like a change of clothes, deodorant, toothbrush, and hairbrush. Keeping these items easily accessible allowed us to get ready for bed quickly and get ready for our day quickly as well.

The lunch bin also sat on top of the platform. It contained tortillas, peanut butter, jelly, fruit, applesauce and other lunch items. It also contained some bulky things like paper towels, plastic bags, ice cream cones, and s'mores fixings.

A week or two into our trip we came up with good systems and routines that helped us stay organized. At night we each knew it was time to clear the stuff that was on the platform so that we could go to bed. We would move the bins and bathroom bags to the cab of the truck so that we had more space to sleep. Then we would brush our teeth and get ready for bed. The last person in the truck would pull on the paracord string on the tailgate to easily close the tailgate. Then that person would reach out and grab the truck cap door, close it, and latch it shut. We both worked to hang the curtains, then used the remote to make sure the truck was locked, turned off the lights, and called it a night.

In the morning, we had a similar routine of making our beds, moving everything from the cab of the truck back to the platform, and getting ready for our day. It would have been nice to have these systems set up earlier in order to keep everything running smoothly and organized, but we had no way of knowing and had to live and learn on the road.

Truck Cab

The majority of our personal belongings stayed in each of our closets. But some things did wind up in other places—like our laptops. They belonged behind the seats in the cab of the truck. We referred to this space as the office.

While on the road, the passenger could easily access her laptop from the office and pass time by backing up photos or typing up the next blog. We also each had a day-hike backpack that was stored in the office. These backpacks had the essentials for hiking, but it also had important things like cameras and wallets. A bonus to having our more expensive items in the office space in the cab was that they were always safe from the weather. And we could simply lock the cab at night and our valuables would be safe.

Between the front seats was a catch-all bin that became known as our entertainment center. Things like charging cords, the transmitter, earbuds, maps, gum, and other random items collected there. I guess it would be considered the "junk draw" of our home on wheels.

Any guesses on what we stored in the glove box? It wasn't gloves, but instead we had a very large first aid kit. It was our medicine cabinet. Everything from Band-Aids and sanitary wipes to ibuprofen and vitamins were kept in the glove box, along with our vehicle's registration, of course.

Our goal from the start was to keep our home on wheels clean and functional. We would accumulate a small collection of trash in the truck, but every day we stopped at a gas station or a park where we could throw it away. We developed the habit of throwing all the trash away every time we left the truck. Neither one of us is a messy person and we both enjoy having an organized living space. This definitely helped us keep a healthy relationship. We didn't have to clean up after each other and we didn't have to ask each other to clean up.

★ *Relationship Tip:* Clean up after yourself!

Chapter 7 Takeaways:

❑ Space is limited so use it wisely.
❑ Store the items that you use regularly in easy to access locations.
❑ Store the items that you don't use regularly in the harder to access locations.
❑ Create barriers to protect your personal space.
❑ Clean up after yourself.

PACKING

from Melissa's perspective

We had to fit many items in our home on wheels and many more items we had to leave behind. From clothes, to camping equipment, to cooking items, there's much to consider. We had to be a little picky, but we still had everything we needed, plus some.

Personal Packing

In our closets, we needed to fit a variety of clothing for a wide range of terrain and weather. For instance, we were swimming in Biscayne, Florida one day. Then less than one week later we were trekking in one-hundred-degree weather in Big Bend, Texas. That same night, we drove across Texas, arriving in New Mexico with the temperature in the thirties. Four weeks later, we were hiking through snow in California, and the next week we were strolling through the Hoh rainforest in Washington.

With all this diversity, the option of layers is essential. We did not bring any bulky coats, we simply added layers on the cold or windy days. Athletic and wool materials kept us dry and warm better than cotton. Sweatshirts, leggings, loose sweatpants, hats, and a wind-breaking rain jacket were all layers we used many times. Of course, if you end up needing more layers, you can always buy some along the way. (Clothes make great souvenirs anyway!)

Here is the packing list we recommend:

Clothing:
- ❏ Rain jacket
- ❏ 2 hoodies
- ❏ 10 t-shirts or tanks
- ❏ Water resistant pants
- ❏ Warm leggings
- ❏ 7 pairs of shorts
- ❏ 5 pairs of pants
- ❏ 14 pairs of socks
- ❏ Lots of underwear
- ❏ Hiking shoes
- ❏ Athletic shoes
- ❏ Flip flops or sandals
- ❏ Belt
- ❏ Hat
- ❏ Swimsuit
- ❏ Winter hat and gloves
- ❏ Sunglasses

Miscellaneous:
- ❏ 2 towels
- ❏ 2 washcloths
- ❏ Laundry soap
- ❏ Bug spray
- ❏ Sunscreen
- ❏ Aloe
- ❏ Vitamins or supplements
- ❏ Pocketknife
- ❏ Cloth or drawstring bag

Hygiene:
- ❑ Toiletry bag
- ❑ Toothbrush and toothpaste
- ❑ Hairbrush and hair accessories
- ❑ Shampoo and conditioner
- ❑ Bar of soap or body wash
- ❑ Razor
- ❑ Hand sanitizer
- ❑ Body wipes
- ❑ Deodorant
- ❑ Lip balm
- ❑ Lotion
- ❑ Nail clippers
- ❑ Tissues

Camping Equipment

We kept camping equipment to a minimum, and we used fewer things than we originally thought we would. For example, we packed a small collapsible aluminum table with us that we thought we would use to cook on, yet it never made it out of the truck.

The platform in the back of the truck was a hard surface to sleep on. So, we each brought two sleeping bags. One was bulky and the other was a backpacking sleeping bag made for cooler weather. With the bulky one, we made "mattresses" by each placing a foam camping mat inside of the sleeping bag. Then on top of those, we laid the backpacking sleeping bag. We each also brought our own pillows and an extra blanket to complete the comfort.

One night we tried to sleep outside in hammocks, but the buzzing of bugs sent us back inside the truck. Even so, it was still nice to have the hammocks as options on warm nights. We chose not to bring a tent.

Our camping equipment necessities:

- ❑ Warm sleeping bag
- ❑ Large sleeping bag (to put the foam mat inside)
- ❑ Foam camping mat(s) (double them up if you like more cushion)
- ❑ Hammock with a bug net
- ❑ Pillow
- ❑ Extra blanket
- ❑ Headlight
- ❑ Day pack with a water bladder
- ❑ Water bottle
- ❑ Fire starter

Additional Items to Keep in The Truck

Some things for the truck we ended up buying along the way. For example, we needed to replace a windshield wiper and turn signal light bulbs. Of course, we needed an oil change too.

A few things you should consider bringing are a set of tools, a first aid kit, and a safe. We appreciated having all of these. The tools came in handy when we needed to change the turn signal light bulbs on the truck. You never know when you'll need some tools! The first aid kit also came in handy and was convenient to get to in the glove box. The small safe was perfect for holding valuable items such as our passports, a handgun, and some extra cash. Most of the time we kept it locked underneath the driver's seat.

One thing that we brought with us that we didn't end up using much was an empty plastic cereal container to use as a trash can. It seemed like a good idea at first, but it turned out to be too inconvenient, bulky, and awkward to access.

Safety and precaution items:
- ❑ Lockable safe
- ❑ Gun
- ❑ Pepper spray
- ❑ Spare keys
- ❑ First aid kit
  - ❑ Ibuprofen
  - ❑ Band-Aids of various sizes
  - ❑ Neosporin
  - ❑ Gauze
- ❑ Jumper cables
- ❑ Toolbox

Travel items:
- ❑ Passport
- ❑ Wallet
- ❑ National park pass
- ❑ Envelope with cash
- ❑ Daily itinerary
- ❑ Any ferry or tour tickets
- ❑ Paper maps (at least one large map of the U.S.)

Technology and entertainment:
- ❑ Laptops and charging cords
- ❑ Extension cord with a power strip
- ❑ Power inverter (see chapter 9)
- ❑ Camera/ GoPro™/ and batteries or chargers
- ❑ USB phone charger
- ❑ Phone mount
- ❑ Headphones
- ❑ A couple of books
- ❑ Index cards (see chapter 12)

Kitchen Equipment

The two things that took up the most space were the cooking items and all the food. Since food is very important to us, our kitchen was important to us, especially since we would cook most of the food ourselves. Thus, we needed a good kitchen set-up, and we did not need much to accomplish our cooking goals.

The most essential piece of our "good kitchen" was a camping stove. When we opened up the stove, the lid stood up and blocked the wind from behind, and two panels acted as wind blockers on either side. These wind blockers were essential to keeping our fire lit on windy days. Our camping stove had two burners—one long burner with a grill grate on top, and one small circular burner. A small propane tank fueled the stove. After attaching the tank to the stove, we used a lighter to ignite a flame.

We also had a small cooler to hold things like butter or fresh vegetables that we picked up from grocery stores along the way. We often did not buy things that needed refrigeration, because we did not want to worry about buying ice. However, buying ice wasn't an issue when we got up to the northern parts of California, Oregon, and Washington. Instead, we packed our cooler with icy snow that we gathered along the way.

Our basic kitchen items included:
- ❏ Camping stove
- ❏ Propane
- ❏ Lighter
- ❏ One small-sized pot
- ❏ One medium-sized pot with a lid
- ❏ One medium-sized skillet
- ❏ Thin plastic cutting board
- ❏ Blender bottle with whisk
- ❏ Can opener
- ❏ Heat resistant serving spoon
- ❏ Rubber spatula

- ❑ Flipper spatula
- ❑ Whisk
- ❑ Pair of tongs
- ❑ Scissors
- ❑ Paring knife
- ❑ Set of measuring cups and spoons
- ❑ Two hot pads
- ❑ Small collapsible cooler

For dishes, we had four sporks, four plastic bowls, three thin stainless-steel plates, and one extra plastic set of silverware. These all got so much use that many of our sporks broke along the way. Actually, one of them broke because I left it somewhere I shouldn't have.

★ **Relationship Tip:** *Be quick to forgive your travel buddy if they accidentally leave dishes on the top of the truck when you drive off.*

Cleaning up after meals was a little tricky at times. We had dish towels, dish soap, a scrub sponge, and a large plastic bin. We sometimes washed dishes with these. If the meal wasn't very messy, we could wipe off our dishes and reuse them before a full wash. Often, we found water spigots or sinks to wash out all our dishes.

Coffee was important to us, so Christina made pour-over coffee on most mornings. We set plastic pour-over drippers (with our coffee and filters inside) directly over our thermoses and poured hot water right in. It was such a treat!

Here is the rest of our kitchen items:
- ❑ 4 sporks
- ❑ 3 plates
- ❑ 4 plastic bowls

- ❑ Extra set of plastic silverware
- ❑ Collapsible roasting sticks
- ❑ Coffee thermoses
- ❑ Plastic pour over coffee drippers
- ❑ Coffee filters
- ❑ Dish drying towels
- ❑ Dish soap
- ❑ Scrub brush/scraper
- ❑ Foil
- ❑ Sandwich bags
- ❑ A few plastic grocery bags
- ❑ 2 large storage bins with lids
- ❑ 2 large open bins
- ❑ 1 medium dish pan
- ❑ 2 shoe box size bins with lids
- ❑ Storage cube bin
- ❑ Non-skid grip shelf liner
- ❑ Travel size broom with dustpan

In the two shoebox-sized bins we kept our cooking utensils and our small dry goods like salt, pepper, sugar, and popcorn. In the two large open bins, we kept the bulkier items such as our pots, pans, and dishes. The one medium dish pan we mainly used for washing dishes. One time we used it for stirring up our home-made caramel popcorn (for our recipe see the appendix).

The two storage bins with lids kept our pantry items sealed up well. One bin kept our breakfast and coffee items stored away, and the other bin kept our pantry items such as our soup cans and any extra instant meals.

Chapter 8 Takeaways:

❑ Pack multiple options for layering clothes in as much wool and athletic material as possible.

❑ You don't need much camping gear when sleeping in your own vehicle, but make sure it's comfy with as many thick camping pads and blankets as you need.

❑ Keep room for emergency items in your vehicle such as tools, first aid kit, and jumper cables.

❑ A propane camping stove and some kitchen basics can take up a lot of space, but they are essential for a budget friendly trip and delicious meals on the road.

CHAPTER 9

PREPARING FOR THE PARKS

from Melissa's perspective

There are many books out there that can tell you how to tackle each park and the best time to do each trail. I will save that education for people who have spent a longer time than us at each park. But here, I can tell you how we recommend generally approaching the parks and which parks take extra planning. In addition, I will share things we brought along with us on the hikes.

Planning around Tours, Ferries, and Excursions

Some national parks offer tours, ferries, or excursions and will require extra planning to participate. Three parks we visited—Dry Tortugas, Channel Islands, and Isle Royale—are all on islands and require ferry rides to access them. To visit them you will have to plan your day around the ferry schedule and look into buying tickets in advance.

Other parks offer cave or cavern tours. You will again need to plan around the tour schedules if you plan to participate, and you may need to purchase tickets in advance. Some of them don't allow access to the underground areas except by a tour guide. Although several national parks have caves or caverns, three parks feature them as their main attraction. These parks are Wind Cave, Mammoth Cave, and Carlsbad Caverns.

A couple other national parks that you may want to plan out beforehand are Mesa Verde and Biscayne. Mesa Verde offers many guided tours to choose from that will walk you through the rich history and culture there. Biscayne is ninety-five percent underwater. In order to fully explore this park, you may want to plan an excursion snorkeling or sailing (or both).

Planning around Crowds

Although crowds and a lack of parking are inevitable at most national parks, there are small things you can do to help. As we previously discussed, we visited the parks in the spring. Avoiding the parks in the summer will help cut down tremendously on the crowds. Avoiding the more popular parks on the weekends will also help.

Even if you visit in the summer or on a weekend, at least make sure you arrive at the park early. When we went to Yellowstone National Park, we were there on a Saturday on June 10th, but we were walking around the hot springs before 8:00 am. We had entire boardwalks to ourselves—it was amazing! One reason that we were able to do this was because we stayed at a camping area within the park. Staying within or nearby the parks will make it even easier to arrive early and beat the crowds.

Planning around the Visitor Centers

We also decided to plan our stops around the national park visitor center's hours. We usually wanted to stop by in order to grab a map, refill on water, or talk to the park rangers. We had to look up when the visitor centers opened and closed in order to do this.

Before we left home, we had researched hikes to do at many of the parks. Yet, towards the end of the trip we hadn't gotten as far with our planning. Instead, we liked to first approach the visitor center and ask the park rangers what hikes they recommended. Then we could tell them just what kinds of trails we were looking for at the park. We asked for pretty views and told them that we were not afraid of hikes with big elevation changes. The rangers were very helpful to us. We recommend asking them for suggestions anytime.

Planning around Hikes

As mentioned in chapter 4, you'll have to discuss with your travel buddy the types of hikes that you both want to do. Now you will have to plan out your visit around those types of hikes. For example, if you want to do longer, more strenuous hikes, you'll want to plan to be at the parks early in the day. For us this was especially true when we got to Big Bend, Death Valley, and Grand Canyon. Even though we visited all these parks in the spring, they were still very hot. Getting a morning start to the trails in these parks was crucial.

Even if it is not hot when you are hiking, if you hike a long trail you still need to plan to be back in time before sunset. One time we were on a long hike and had to almost sprint all the way back down to the parking lot because we were told the sun would be setting soon. Not quite the type of hike we had in mind!

Planning for the Hikes

Without overpacking, you will want to be well-prepared for your hike. We always liked to have an extra snack on us and bring more than enough water. We got better as we went with predicting how much we would eat and drink on a long hike. Towards the beginning of our trip there was one time in particular that I wished I had packed more water.

★ **Relationship Tip:** *Bringing and sharing extra water with your travel buddy when she didn't bring enough will make her very grateful for you.*

Here is what we packed with us in our day-hike backpacks:
- ❑ Large filled water bottle or water bladder
- ❑ Snacks
- ❑ Park map
- ❑ Compass
- ❑ Light raincoat or hoodie (depending on the predicted weather and temperatures)
- ❑ Camera or phone
- ❑ Mini first aid kit
- ❑ Sunglasses
- ❑ Hat
- ❑ Pocketknife
- ❑ Lip balm
- ❑ Hand sanitizer
- ❑ Sunscreen
- ❑ Tissues
- ❑ Flashlight or headlamp
- ❑ Whistle
- ❑ Keys
- ❑ Wallet

Some parks recommend having bear spray with you on hikes also. You can ask in the visitor center, and many will have some for rent or purchase.

Chapter 9 Takeaways:

- ❏ For national parks with caves, ferries, or tours, you will need to plan your visit in advance. These include:
  - ❏ Dry Tortugas, Florida
  - ❏ Channel Islands, California
  - ❏ Isle Royale, Michigan
  - ❏ Wind Cave, South Dakota
  - ❏ Mammoth Cave, Kentucky
  - ❏ Carlsbad Caverns, New Mexico
- ❏ You can best avoid crowds by:
  - ❏ Visiting parks in the off-season
  - ❏ Arriving early in the morning
  - ❏ Avoiding the busiest parks on weekends
- ❏ Ask inside the visitor centers for suggestions on what to see and hike within the parks.
- ❏ Consider the distance of the hike, heat of the day, and daylight when planning out when to hike.
- ❏ Be prepared with a well-supplied day pack.

PREPARING MEALS FROM OUR TAILGATE

from Melissa's perspective

C ooking your own food while traveling takes some creativity and planning—but nothing too complicated. Often, it's as simple as warming up a can of soup. It's a slight mindset shift. Especially when you are used to having a stocked kitchen with a stove and refrigerator. But now, you have a tiny camp stove, a few dry ingredients, and a jug of water. If you plan to cook much of your own food, you will want to keep some basic items stocked, and have plenty of options for breakfasts, lunches, and dinners. We have many ideas and even some recipes to share with you.

Water

Many of the meals we cooked required water. And of course, you will want some water on hand anyway for rehydrating. But if you have limited space as we did, it is not practical to store gallons of water in the truck to use for drinking and cooking. Yet we did find it very practical to consistently keep one gallon of water filled. I also recommend having large water bottles and water bladders to also fill up. We constantly refilled our water bottles, so we rarely had to dip into the gallon of water except for when cooking. There are multiple ways to fill up on water while on a road trip.

National Parks are great at having water stations at their visitor centers. Thus, these can be your main filling stations. On a trip like this, you will visit one every single day. Every time we made it to a new park, we would first stop by the visitor center and bring our water bottles and our jug of water with us. If we had a long day planned before we would visit the next park, we would fill them up again before we left. It was a great habit to form, and it never left us thirsty.

Paid campgrounds are another place you can fill up your jug along the way. Although we did not stay at many, they have great access to water. If you take a day driving where you will not be at a national park, staying the night at a campground is a perfect way to be sure you will still have enough.

Whenever you stop for food at a fast-food restaurant, you can always request water and pour the filled cup into your water bottle. Of course, filling up a gallon of water here doesn't make sense, but it is a good way to top off water bottles.

We found that the longer we were on the road, the more we found ourselves looking for various ways to get water. This became a natural instinct, and it was not hard to find when looking. This wasn't something that required specific planning for us. Yet if need be or you are nervous about it, simply store some extra water or re-stock at the grocery store along the way.

Making Food on the Road

Oh, the places we cooked! Having such a portable kitchen allowed us to cook meals in some remarkable places. Most of the time we would pull out the stove and cook on the tailgate, but sometimes we cooked on the ground in a parking lot. Occasionally, we would be in a scenic place and we would place the stove on a table or a short rock wall nearby to enjoy the amazing views while we cooked.

I do have to say, sometimes when we were cooking in unique places, we got some strange looks—especially in parking lots. A few times we even had some people take pictures of us like we were part of the tourist attraction in the area! In times like these, you could often hear us reassure each other, "Is this weird?" "No, this is perfectly normal." We honestly got used to the looks, and by the end of the trip, it did feel normal.

★ **Relationship Tip:** *Regularly re-assure each other that you are both "normal" when doing strange, yet necessary things.*

Basics

We stocked up on many basic items before our trip and replenished these when needed along the way. Here is a grocery list of helpful items you could almost always find in our "pantry":

- ❏ A few favorite seasonings
- ❏ Brown sugar
- ❏ Butter
- ❏ Canola oil
- ❏ Cinnamon
- ❏ Honey
- ❏ Maple syrup
- ❏ One gallon of water
- ❏ Parmesan cheese
- ❏ Popcorn salt
- ❏ Powdered milk
- ❏ Salt and pepper

Breakfast Ideas

In addition to the above basics, for breakfast foods we would often stock up on the following:

- ❏ Granola/ or another cereal
- ❏ Individual boxes of milk (that don't require refrigeration)
- ❏ Grits or cream of wheat
- ❏ Ground coffee
- ❏ Muffin mix (just add water type)
- ❏ Oatmeal
- ❏ Pancake mix (just add water)

The oatmeal and grits were quite nice for cold mornings. We warmed up enough hot water for both coffee and oatmeal. Then we poured the hot water right into our bowls holding the oats or grits. We always added extra toppings to complete the hearty breakfast. We liked brown sugar, powdered milk, cinnamon, or even peanut butter.

We cooked up the muffin mix like pancakes, but these "pancakes" don't need any syrup. They come in a variety of delicious flavors and are nice and quick to cook up. See our recipe in the appendix.

For pancakes, we enjoyed the "just add water" variety of the brand Hungry Jack® pancakes. As a special treat, we cooked up some apples with butter, sugar, and cinnamon for a delicious topping. (See our apple topping recipe in the appendix.)

Lunch and Snack Ideas

We were often driving or hiking during lunchtime. So, lunches for us often consisted of quick options and snack foods. Items we packed for snacks and lunches included:

- ❏ Applesauce packages

- ❏ Beef jerky
- ❏ Canned chicken or tuna
- ❏ Canned fruit
- ❏ Dried fruit
- ❏ Fresh fruit (like bananas, apples, cherries, grapes)
- ❏ Fresh veggies (like carrots and snap peas)
- ❏ Granola bars
- ❏ Jelly
- ❏ Peanut butter
- ❏ Mayo packets
- ❏ Popcorn kernels
- ❏ Salty snacks (like pretzels or crackers)
- ❏ Tortilla wraps or a loaf of bread
- ❏ Trail mixes

Tortilla wraps were easy to make on the go. We often made mayonnaise chicken or tuna wraps, or peanut butter and jelly wraps. When we had a long day or two of driving ahead of us, we enjoyed buying fresh veggies to snack on. We always had to eat these within a day or two of purchasing them as they do not do well sitting in the car for too long. Our favorite snack was definitely popcorn. We would often pop it in our little pan on our stove after breakfast to enjoy it later on the road.

Dinner Ideas

The ingredients we packed for dinners included:
- ❏ Canned soup
- ❏ Canned veggies
- ❏ Fresh veggies
- ❏ Instant mashed potatoes
- ❏ Ramen noodles
- ❏ Rice
- ❏ Baked beans

- ❑ Variety of quick stovetop meals
- ❑ Stir fry ingredients

Knorr® has multiple pasta sides and entrees that cook on the stove in less than ten minutes (and only cost about $1.00 each). Often, they call for milk which is when we used our powdered milk mixed with water. We also mixed in canned chicken and canned veggies with these pasta entrees to make a more complete meal. Some of our favorite Knorr meals were their Alfredo, Teriyaki Noodles, Chicken Fettuccini, and Creamy Chicken. These meals were extremely convenient.

Tacos were another dinner that was easy to whip up. We used our tortillas, canned chicken, baked beans, and rice. Sometimes we even had some salsa on hand.

Another quick meal we made was what we called "ramen bombs." This was simply ramen noodles mixed with instant mashed potatoes. I know the name (and perhaps the ingredients) doesn't sound the most appetizing. But believe me, after a long hike these quick calories are so regenerating. You'll have to trust me on this one.

★ **Relationship Tip:** *Keep each other from getting hangry by preparing quick, filling meals after long hikes.*

Sometimes we were able to buy some fresh veggies and cook them up the same night or the following day. It was always refreshing when we were able to make dinner with fresh ingredients. One Saturday we even hit up a farmer's market and purchased some delicious fresh produce that way.

Sweet Treat Ideas

We are big fans of a little something sweet. Of course, we had fun snacks in the car like M&M'S™ chocolate and caramel candy, and we often enjoyed stopping for ice cream. We even came up with some fun ways to make desserts. For example, we made cookies, peach cobbler, pudding, and caramel popcorn. The only items needed for these that weren't already on previous lists are the following:

- ❑ Chocolate chip cookie mix (We used the Betty Crocker™ brand.)
- ❑ Instant pudding box
- ❑ Can of peaches
- ❑ Baking soda
- ❑ Marshmallows
- ❑ Graham crackers
- ❑ Chocolate bars

For the chocolate chip cookies, we mixed in the oil or butter (and water if necessary) and fried it as one big cookie in our skillet. Since we didn't carry eggs with us we did not add any, but the cookies still came together just fine. They were best eaten with a fork though, as they are quite messy this way.

For the instant pudding, we divided the pudding powder into two sandwich bags, added some powdered milk, and poured cold water in the bag. We carefully shook it around for a while until it set. This works best when you find a very cold water source and can make it right away. If the water is too warm, it won't set. Squeeze the pudding out of the bag and enjoy!

Recipes

Towards the end of our trip, we were getting more creative. We invented some new (and remembered some old) recipes to try out on our little stove. We used the ingredients we had with us. Three of our favorites were peach cobbler, caramel popcorn, and an apple syrup pancake topping. The peach cobbler recipe is below. Check out all of our recipes in our appendix in the back of the book.

Peach Cobbler

Time: About twenty minutes from start to finish
Cooking Tools Required:
- Camp stove with propane and a lighter
- Saucepan with lid
- Mixing bowl
- Heat-resistant serving spoon
- Fork
- Can opener

Extra Necessity:
- Grocery or convenience store nearby

Ingredients:
- 1 can of peaches in syrup
- Pancake mix
- Oats
- Brown Sugar
- Cinnamon
- Butter

Directions:
1) Place the peaches with syrup into the saucepan and whisk in a few spoonfuls of pancake mix.
2) Light the stove and place a lid on the pan. Let the mixture warm and thicken over medium-low heat. Stir occasionally.
3) While that's warming up, mix in a separate bowl the following: a couple of handfuls of oats, a spoonful of brown sugar, a sprinkle of cinnamon, and a couple tablespoons of butter.
4) When the peaches are hot and bubbly, sprinkle this crumble mixture over the peaches.

5) Place the lid back on the pot and move the pot from the fast cooking burner to the slow cooking burner (or reduce heat if that's an option for you).
6) Let simmer on the low burner for about five minutes.
7) While it's simmering, send your travel buddy inside the grocery store to buy vanilla ice cream to enjoy with the cobbler.

Serves two hungry hikers.

Chapter 10 Takeaways:

- ❑ Fill up your water bottles and jugs daily at national park water stations or campgrounds.
- ❑ Stock up on many basic food items before you go.
- ❑ Look for "just add water" mixes to bring on your trip for convenient meals.
- ❑ For breakfast, think of quick meals. Granola with boxed milk, pancakes, oatmeal, grits, and muffin mixes are easy choices.
- ❑ Keep multiple snack choices in the vehicle for lunches and long drives.
- ❑ Cooking a hearty dinner after long days of hiking is so refreshing and can be as easy as a ten-minute meal with Knorr® packets or soup.

~⊚~ CHAPTER 11 ~⊚~

ACCESSING WI-FI AND OUTLETS

from Melissa's perspective

E very so often when you are in remote places, your phone reception might not cut it (especially if you have the phone service I do). Sometimes we would need Wi-Fi to look up where to sleep for the night. Other times we used Wi-Fi to video call our family and friends back home or post our blog from our laptops. We downloaded songs, podcasts, and audiobooks on Wi-Fi. I used it to send postcards via an online app. We did so much on Wi-Fi that even with unlimited data plans, it was still valuable.

We also needed outlets in order to do all these things on our laptops and phones and in order to keep any other gadgets and batteries charged. As we traveled, we quickly learned the best and worst places for Wi-Fi, and we became quite creative in finding outlets. Pretty soon, we started spotting outlets in so many weird places that we wouldn't have noticed if we hadn't been in the practice of looking for them.

Accessing Wi-Fi

It's fairly easy to find some good places to connect to the internet. Sometimes it can even be a wonderful break to enjoy some coffee or food while on Wi-Fi. We visited many local and chain coffee shops, fast-food restaurants, a few national parks, and a public library. We found that many coffee shops tended to have better Wi-Fi than fast-food restaurants.

Over a dozen national parks offer Wi-Fi in their visitor centers or lodges. These parks include the Grand Canyon, Yellowstone, Great Smoky Mountains, Glacier, Bryce, and Everglades. Many of these lodges are beautiful and have the best atmospheres for working while on Wi-Fi. After days of driving and hiking, relaxing in a national park lodge while blogging provided a great change of pace.

Accessing Outlets

Sometimes you might need an outlet even if you can't access Wi-Fi. This is true especially in moments when you need to charge your phone, laptop, or camera batteries. Of course, the places mentioned above all have outlets. But, in addition to those, I also recommend having a power inverter that can run off of your vehicle's battery. We used it only when the truck was running so as to not drain the battery. But this allows you to charge a laptop, a GoPro™ camera, a smartwatch and anything else you want to charge on the go. This was quite helpful to us.

Consider also bringing a small extension cord with a power strip on the end. We had one with us, and it allowed us to charge four additional things at once. Additionally, if the outlet we needed wasn't close to a seating area it was nice to have the extension cord part of it too. Bringing this proved very helpful to us!

Soon you'll become a pro at finding outlets and may start seeing them everywhere. We noticed them at gas stations, outside random buildings, in restaurants, and on ceilings in coffee shops. (Still to this day I find myself finding outlets in strange places.)

One evening as we were about to head out of a park, we got excited to see a three-sided concrete shelter with outlets inside. Because of this discovery, we spent the evening right there. We quickly cooked up some food. Then we wrapped ourselves in a blanket, with a bowl of soup and worked on our laptops right there on the concrete ground. We were sure we were living it up at that moment!

★   *Relationship Tip: Doing only normal things together is boring. Being a little out of the ordinary every once in a while is good for your relationship.*

Chapter 11 Takeaways:

❑   Remember that Wi-Fi may be necessary for when your phone has no service.

❑   Stop at coffee shops, fast-food restaurants, libraries, or national park visitor centers or lodges to use their Wi-Fi and outlets.

❑   Buy a power inverter to use when your vehicle is running.

~&~ CHAPTER 12 ~&~

ENTERTAINMENT

from Christina's perspective

While on the road trip we were usually doing one of the following: driving, hiking, eating, or sleeping. Before leaving on the trip, we had all sorts of entertainment planned—mostly for while on the road. We were anticipating over three hundred hours of driving time! So, having entertainment while driving was necessary. But we didn't have much planned for entertainment while hiking. While on the trip we tried to get creative and we were constantly trying to find new topics to discuss. We will share our ideas for entertainment while on the road and on the trail.

Entertainment on the Road

What Free Time?

As we were planning the road trip, we were anticipating having a lot of free time. With all the driving we were going to do, surely we would need to bring along things to entertain ourselves, right? We imagined that we would have all the time in the world for leisure activities. Activities like reading books, listening to audio books, writing letters, and calling back home. Not long into the trip we realized that these leisure activities would be a little scarcer than originally planned. There was almost always something to do, and we were almost always busy.

While on the road, the driver was obviously busy driving. What we didn't expect was that the passenger was almost always busy too. We didn't plan out every single detail before taking off on the road trip. So, whoever was sitting in the passenger's seat was most often researching our next destination.

Researching the next destination was actually pretty time consuming. It was especially time consuming to research a place to park for the night. (see chapter 14 for more information on finding places to park for the night.) After finding the next destination, the passenger would pull up directions for the driver and make sure the driver was all set. Being willing to serve each other by getting directions, a snack, or whatever the other may need helps to fuel a healthy relationship.

★ *Relationship Tip: Look for opportunities to serve each other.*

After the driver was set, the passenger was able to take some time to do whatever she needed to do. Which was most often typing up the next blog post and backing up photos on her laptop. Before the trip, neither one of us had written any blogs, but we both agreed that it would be fun to blog our travels. Our families and friends also told us that they would love to read about our travels and that they would live vicariously through us. So, why not blog?

Blogging

Documenting our road trip through blogging became a huge part of our "entertainment" and consumed a lot of our free time. We definitely underestimated how much time we would spend documenting our travels. In our minds, typing up a blog wouldn't take very long. We both enjoyed writing, so we were all for it and excited to document our travels and share our stories. But blogging also added the need to find Wi-Fi from time to time to post our blogs online.

We are so glad that we took the time to write about and share our adventure through blogging. This was a once in a lifetime kind of trip and we wanted to document all that we could so that we wouldn't forget anything. It was worth it to us, and we would definitely recommend documenting your trip in some form of writing. It's so fun to read through and relive your adventures.

Downloads

Blogging wasn't the only thing that we did for car ride entertainment. Before we left on the trip we downloaded all sorts of things like audiobooks, movies, music, and more. We spent quite some time listening to audiobooks while we drove. It was a great way to pass some time.

We did watch several movies throughout the trip. A few of the movies that we had downloaded we had both watched so many times that we could envision the movies and just listen to the audio. So we did that several times on the road. The driver was only able to listen to the movie and envision it but the passenger would actually watch the movie. With some of the movies that we hadn't previously watched, we would make a movie night of it. We would enjoy a salty snack with our movie while all nice and cozy in bed. We only had a couple movie nights, but we greatly enjoyed the relaxation. It was fun to disconnect and just relax.

At times, the road trip felt like a marathon. Just constant go, go, go. Mixing up the driving and hiking with some relaxing helped us avoid burnout. Sure, we could have been making progress by driving or we could have been hiking in some beautiful place. But chilling together and doing "nothing" was good for our mental health. It was also a good way to give ourselves quiet time. I would definitely recommend that you bring something that is relaxing for you and your travel buddy.

Often on Sundays we would try to download a sermon from one of our hometown churches. This was a great way to use our time on the road. We both found it relaxing and rejuvenating to hear from God's word while traveling. This also helped give me a better perspective and reminded me to thank God for the opportunity that He had given us, and it reminded me to look for Him in our day to day life on the road and on the trails. It made us feel at home to hear from our hometown pastors even though we were miles away!

Listening to music was definitely our favorite form of entertainment. It was also the easiest and most convenient. Before the trip, we both signed up for Apple Music's two-month free trial. This was genius. We thought that the road trip would be the perfect time to use it. We both downloaded a small playlist of our favorite songs and we listened to them quite frequently. We also created a lot of playlists together.

We had a playlist that reminded us of different states and this list grew as the trip went on. This playlist consisted of songs like John Denver's "Take Me Home Country Road" and Little Texas' "God Bless Texas." Throughout the trip, this playlist also gained a lot of patriotic music. There was just something about driving all over the United States that made us feel more patriotic and proud to be an American. For me, traveling all over America made me more appreciative of the sacrifices that are made so that I can live here in this beautiful country.

Our favorite playlist that we created was our road trip theme song playlist. We listened to it just about every day. It had so many good songs like, Willie Nelson's "On the Road Again," Johnny Cash's "I've Been Everywhere," Avicii's "The Days," and High Valley's "Memory Makin." Usually we would listen to it in the morning and it would get us pumped for the day's adventures. It was a great way to start off our driving for the day. But we quickly had the playlists memorized and would end up listening to the radio for the majority of the time.

Radio

One of our most widely used forms of entertainment for us was the radio. I mostly listen to country music, and Melissa likes a variety of genres but is more selective within those genres. To keep us both entertained we would frequently switch radio stations. When we couldn't find a station that either of us liked, we would listen to a random song on a random station. Then, we would go to the next station and listen to another random song. Sometimes this was entertaining just because we got to listen to a very wide variety of music. It definitely got us to listen to songs that we would have never heard otherwise, some of which were very strange to us.

The strangest station and song that we found was when we turned on the radio in Death Valley National Park. The one and only station in the valley was playing yodeling. That was a first for us. I had no idea that yodeling was offered on the radio. There were several times out West in the middle of nowhere where there were no stations available at all on the radio. That was always a little disappointing. That's when we would turn to our downloads again.

We were thankful that we had such a wide variety and options for on-the-road music. But you can only listen to so much music before it gets old and boring. When we were nearing the end of the road trip, we were definitely music and "radioed" out! It's hard to admit it, but as we were nearing the end of our trip, the commercials on the radio were becoming more entertaining than the music. That is because the same music was offered pretty much everywhere in the United States. But the commercials varied much more. With all that being said, the radio has its place and can be quite entertaining. But you can never download too much music before you hit the road.

Index Cards

Something we enjoyed on especially long drives was pulling out the box of index cards that had conversation starters on them. Before the trip, our family and friends wrote a bunch of random topics to discuss and questions to ask on the index cards. They were great! I would highly recommend asking your friends and family to do the same for you and your travel buddy. I'm sure you can look up conversation starters too. But it was nice to have the personal touch from our family and friends. Because they know us, they were able to ask questions that were more relatable to us.

Index card examples:

From Grace: *If you could live in any time era, when would it be?*

From Jenny: *If your life were a movie who would play you and what would the title be?*

From Alina: *What has been the highlight of your trip so far?*

From David: *If you could make one species of animals extinct what would you choose?*

From Jessica: *Share an embarrassing moment about an older sibling.*

The conversation starter from Jessica (my youngest sister) was one that really got us talking. She asked us to share an embarrassing story about an *older* sibling thinking that because she was *younger* that she was in the clear. Her index card prompted us to share any embarrassing story that we could think of! We were both laughing so hard that we were crying! It was probably not the safest situation to be in tears and laughing so hard while driving. But we managed to pull it together eventually.

Entertainment on the Trail

On every single hike we were taking photos and enjoying the scenery of course, but we also needed stuff to talk about and do while we were on the trail. We kind of ran out of things to talk about after about the first week of traveling together. Honestly, I heard many of Melissa's stories so many times and could repeat them back to her word for word. I'm not exaggerating! Listen to the repetitive stories if that's what keeps your travel buddy happy. It probably won't hurt you. But, for the sanity of us both, we had to get creative and find ways to talk about new things.

★ *Relationship Tip: Listen to the repetitive stories if that's what keeps your travel buddy happy. It probably won't hurt you.*

Talking about the Parks

An obvious topic of discussion was the national parks. We would randomly ask each other, "What's been your favorite hike or view so far?" We would also go park by park and list our favorite view, hike, or memory from each. We also made a game out of listing the parks to each other. We had them listed on our phones and would see if we could list them all and list them in the order that we visited them. It was a fun little memory game for the two of us.

Memory Game

About halfway through our trip, I taught Melissa a memory game. It's a simple game and nothing that exciting. But we were desperate for something to talk about while hiking and we thought it was fun. The first person simply says, "I'm going on a trip and I am bringing..." and then they choose a random object like a "hat." Then the next person says, "I'm going on a trip and I'm bringing a hat," and then they choose a random object. You continue back and forth, and eventually you have a long list of items. Whoever catches the other person leaving an object out or listing the items out of order, wins!

Phone Contacts "Game"

Toward the end of the trip we were getting desperately low on new things to talk about while on the trail. Melissa and I came up with a "game" where one of us picks a random contact in the other person's phone, and then they had to share how they met and share a story about that person. For example, one of us would say, "Who is the first contact that starts with the letter T?" And then they would proceed to tell the other person all about that contact. We actually got to know a lot more about each other this way. This "game" led us to share so many stories that would have never come up otherwise.

★ **Relationship Tip:** *There's always something new to learn about each other. The trick is finding the key to unlock the stories.*

Talking Futures

Fairly often our conversation led to us dreaming about our futures, and then discussing (in as much detail as possible) things like: What is your dream home and property? What is your dream family? What is your dream job? Who are your role models? Who has had the biggest impact on your life? It's always fun to dream a little and envision that perfect future and share our goals with each other. Discussing our role models led us to dig a little deeper into each other's personal lives. We were always learning about each other and becoming closer friends by talking about our future plans, hopes, and dreams.

Food

One of our most popular topics to discuss while hiking was food. We would sometimes ban food as a topic of discussion. Especially when we were on long hikes and when we were hungry. It was plain cruel on those occasions. But on shorter hikes, or when our stomachs were satisfied, we would talk about our options for dinner as well as try to brainstorm new recipes with the ingredients that we had on hand. Our favorite invention was the peach cobbler recipe that came together while we were hiking in the Hoh Rainforest!

Chapter 12 Takeaways:

On the road entertainment:
- ❏ Document your travels by writing a blog or journal
- ❏ Phone calls
- ❏ Write letters and postcards
- ❏ Audiobooks
- ❏ Movies
- ❏ Music apps
- ❏ Sermons
- ❏ Podcasts
- ❏ Radio
- ❏ Index cards

On the trail entertainment:
- ❏ Reminiscing travels
- ❏ Memory games
- ❏ Phone contact game
- ❏ Talk future plans, hopes, and dreams
- ❏ Talk food

~ﾷ© CHAPTER 13 ©ﾷ~

TRAVELING SAFELY

from Christina's perspective

T hroughout our trip, we always tried to avoid any potentially risky or dangerous situations. I must say we did a good job at it. But we took lots of safety measures. And I mean a lot of safety measures! Let's take a look at how we kept things safe in regards to our vehicle, people approaching us, and how we took personal protection.

Safety Measures for Your Vehicle

Vehicle Knowledge

Before going on a road trip like ours, it is important to know as much as you can about the condition of your vehicle. For as long as my parents owned the truck, they had no major issues with it, but we needed to be sure that everything was good to go for over 16,000 miles.

Since Melissa and I are not mechanically inclined, we took the truck into a shop to get it checked out and tuned up. Nothing major needed done, but we did get new tires and an oil change to keep things running smoothly and to hopefully prevent any issues on the road. We knew that about halfway through our trip we would need an oil change. So, we made sure we allowed for at least half a day for that and also had a mechanic check the truck over.

Know How to Change a Tire

Several years before the road trip I had watched my dad change a tire, but I had never changed a tire myself. So before Melissa and I embarked on a 16,000 plus mile road trip, my dad thought it would be wise to give me a quick demonstration on how to change a tire. This made me aware of everything that I would need and where I could find it. Before a road trip it is smart to check your vehicle for the proper tools and check the condition of your spare tire.

Extra Keys

When my family first purchased the Chevy Colorado truck it came with four keys! Four keys is a little overkill, but we found it to be very nice to have spare keys. Melissa and I each had a key, we kept a key in the truck, and the last key we left at home. In addition to each having a key for the truck we each had a key that locked the cap. We each tried to always have our keys on us, decreasing the chances of both of us locking our keys in the vehicle.

Always Lock Your Vehicle

Always lock your vehicle! We always locked the cap and cab of the truck before we left it. Sometimes it was annoying to have to lock and unlock the cap especially because we were in and out of it so often. But we locked it anyway and we never had any issue with anything getting stolen.

Roadside Assistance

In case we did happen to lock our keys in the car or have some other vehicle issue we had AAA for backup. My parents added me to their AAA policy before the trip. It was nice to know that if we had any issues and needed a tow that we were covered. Melissa and I never had to call for help, thankfully.

Gas Up

Before the trip, all our friends and family were constantly reminding us to gas up often! We heard it so much that it kind of became a joke where people would call us and quickly remind us to fill up. Though in all seriousness, it was good advice. Especially out West! Gas stations are few and far between out there in the desert. We almost always tried to stay above ¼ of a tank. There were a few times out West where we were a little concerned, but we ended up being fine. We were a little nervous at times but right when we were getting close to empty, we came across another gas station. It felt like they were perfectly placed for us. So, fill up when you can!

We also tried to end the day with a mostly full tank of gas. That way we had one less thing to worry about in the morning. We always had the most energy and were more alert in the morning. So it was nice to get up and start driving and cover as much ground as possible without having to stop. A full tank of gas could get us about 4 hours of freeway driving. So filling up at ¼ of a tank (after three hours) was a good distance to drive before stopping again. Because when it came time to fill up again, we were ready to stretch our legs, use the restroom, grab a snack, and switch drivers.

Drive Safely

While on the road, the passenger was always acting as the driver's assistant. For the safety of everyone, the driver's only task was to drive. The passenger was tasked with bringing up directions, helping them get snacks, and if need be, keeping the driver awake and alert. This prevented the driver from having to multi-task while driving. Safety first!

Also, always follow the speed limit! Speeding is a great way to cause injury, mess up your schedule by getting pulled over, and increase your expenses with a ticket. If you've ever gotten a speeding ticket, you know that they are expensive and no fun whatsoever. Though one of us should have gotten a speeding ticket on the road trip, neither one of us actually got one. We got pulled over and it messed up our schedule quite a bit. But we had a generous and understanding officer that chose not to write up a ticket. This incident kept us from speeding (too much) for the rest of our trip.

On the Road Encounters

Try Not to Draw Attention

We tried to be quiet and not draw attention to ourselves. But we can't help but make a scene and draw attention to ourselves while we are washing dishes in a public bathroom or cooking dinner in a random parking lot. It's not normal to see people doing this. On many occasions we had people walk up to us and start up a conversation. And we understood, it's not every day that you see people cooking dinner on a tailgate in a parking lot.

Encountering People

We had a man approach us in Colorado who asked us when we would be heading up the coast of California. We both thought to ourselves, *"Wait. How in the world does this stranger know where we were going?"* Still puzzled at how he knew this and trying to be as vague as possible, we told him that our plan was in fact to drive north through California within the next several weeks.

After freaking us out with his knowledge of our plans, he then told us that he had seen our map in the dash of the truck. He had also noticed our Ohio license plate and was curious to hear about our travels. We chatted with this man and his wife for a bit and this put our minds at ease. It turns out they weren't out there stalking us! But this was a good reminder to us to be more careful about where we put our map and plans for our trip.

Most of the time the people that came up to us were very nice and were simply curious and interested to hear what in the world we were doing! We met people on hikes, in parking lots while cooking, on long ferry rides, at campgrounds, and all over. Most of the time people were excited to hear what we were up to and they were very generous toward us. A couple that we met on a ferry in Florida offered us their house for a night. A stranger in Arizona helped us with our blinker that wasn't working. Someone gave us homemade New York maple syrup after chatting with us in a Utah parking lot. And after offering some of our breakfast to a fellow traveler in Colorado, he restocked us with food, fuel, and water. We were overwhelmed by the generosity of strangers all over the United States. We encountered so many good people throughout our road trip and are so very thankful for each and every one of them.

Be on Guard

First of all, we were always on guard and aware of our surroundings. We weren't paranoid that something bad could happen at any moment. But we were always aware of what was going on around us. If someone approached one of us the other one would come over as well. And we always stood facing toward the individual that approached us and we never turned our back toward them. We wanted to keep an eye on them. You can never be too cautious. Always know where your travel buddy is and look out for one another.

★ **Relationship Tip:** *Always look out for one another.*

Secret Hand Signals

There were times that we did feel a little uncomfortable with the person that approached us. After one occasion when someone approached us and we felt uncomfortable, we decided to come up with hand signals. This way we could secretly communicate with one another and tell one another whether we were comfortable with the situation. This method proved to be very helpful for us. We got pretty good at reading each other's mind as the trip went on. But sometimes it was hard to tell what the other person was thinking, and we were very thankful to have set up the hand signals.

The hand signals were nothing complicated and nothing extremely noticeable. If we felt comfortable with the situation, we made sure our hands were open and relaxed. If we were uncomfortable with the situation then we had a hand more tense and almost in a fist. Most of the time we were okay with the situation and we truly enjoyed chatting with the individuals that came up to us.

But if we felt uncomfortable, we tried to end the conversation and move on—-even if only one of us was uncomfortable. If one of us had a bad feeling about the situation then the other person supported her feelings and did what she could to help end the conversation—even though she may not share the same feelings.

★ **Relationship Tip:** *Be supportive of each other's feelings even if you don't feel the same way.*

Personal Safety Measures

Knives

In addition to the hand signals we both had pocketknives. A little pocketknife probably wouldn't do that much good, but we had them just in case. I'm happy to report that we only used the pocketknives to open up packages of food and to spread cream cheese on our bagels.

Pepper Spray

Also, I had pepper spray within reach almost all the time. The can of pepper spray went wherever I went. I always kept it close. It was kept in either the driver's side door on the truck, in my day pack, or in the box between our beds. Only once did I feel threatened enough to grab it. But thankfully we never needed to use it.

Location Tracking App

Another safety measure that we had was an app that tracks the location of your phone. Melissa installed the tracking app on her phone mostly to give our parents peace of mind. Melissa almost always kept location turned "on" on her phone so that our family could see our location. There was one time along the

Rio Grande when Melissa's phone was running low on battery and she wanted the remaining battery power for taking photos. So she turned off location for a little while, and later we found out that turning off location right next to the border of Mexico made for some rather concerned parents. Oops!

★ **Relationship Tip:** *Try not to give your parents a heart attack. That would definitely hurt your relationship with them.*

At one point along the trip, we were struggling to find a place that we could park for the night, and my aunt pulled up our location and tried to help us out. It was nice to know that our families were there to help and were able to look out for us through the app. Only once did we wish that we didn't have the app. We were trying to make our arrival back home a surprise but having the app made it difficult. We ended up turning location "off" on Melissa's phone so that they couldn't track us. But that led to suspicion because we had no real reason to have our location turned off. All in all, the app was very helpful.

Concealed Carry Weapons Permit

The most extreme safety measure that we took was having a gun with us on the road trip. I grew up around guns and had always wanted to get my concealed carry weapons (CCW) permit. The road trip gave me a good reason to actually go and complete the course. I did so and then purchased a 9mm Ruger LC9s. Though I am beyond grateful that I never had to use it, I am also glad to have had it for security and the peace of mind of knowing I could defend myself if need be.

Melissa did not have a CCW permit, so I was the only one carrying. But just as a precaution before leaving, Melissa came over to my house (out in the country) and shot the gun a few times and familiarized herself with it. When I wasn't carrying the gun, it was stored in a small safe under the driver's seat. The safe was always easily accessible and was cabled to the seat frame in the truck. Before heading out on the road trip I researched which states in the U.S. honors Ohio State CCW laws to make sure I didn't carry where I was not supposed to.

Carrying a gun might not be for everyone, and I understand that. Many see carrying a gun as unnecessary or perhaps over-protective. But we were comforted to know that we could defend ourselves on the road. Imagine how someone with bad intentions would see two women living alone on the road. Kind of vulnerable? An easy target? Not us! Between our phones, our knives, pepper spray, and my gun, we were pretty well prepared!

Self Defense Classes

I also had eight years of mixed martial arts training. So this also helped me feel prepared to defend myself if necessary. And that was a comfort to me. Who knows if I would win or not if I were attacked. But I would not go down without a fight!

Our Faith

And finally, we know that God was looking out for us and that he granted us safety while traveling. We were often asking for His protection, and we know that our support group back home was also praying for us and our safety. We know that God had a hand in this trip, and we saw that on many occasions. We were able to complete the trip with no problems, and we had a great time.

Here are a few other examples of how God had His hand in our travels: The day after we left Texas there was a tornado that touched down. We were unaware that the high winds we experienced could have been dangerous. We were not harmed. We never had any major vehicle issues. We managed to dodge flooding in Arkansas and numerous forest fires around the country. And neither one of us got hurt or sick while on the road.

Chapter 13 Takeaways:

- ❑ Know your vehicle
- ❑ Know how to change a tire and know where's the spare tire and tools are located
- ❑ Have spare keys
- ❑ Always lock your vehicle
- ❑ Get roadside assistance
- ❑ Gas up often
- ❑ Drive safely
- ❑ Don't speed
- ❑ Create a way to secretly communicate with your travel buddy like hand signals
- ❑ Carry a pocketknife
- ❑ Carry pepper spray
- ❑ Get your concealed carry weapons permit
- ❑ Purchase a safe for storing valuables
- ❑ Take self-defense classes
- ❑ Download a location tracking app
- ❑ Have faith and pray (God is the best safety measure of all times)

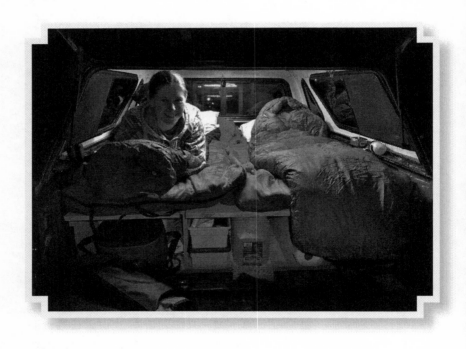

ᐱᐱ Chapter 14 ᐱᐱ

SLEEPING IN A TRUCK

from Melissa's perspective

A good night of sleep is essential when you're hiking or driving all day long. Along the way, we found many peaceful places to park and sleep. But as you can imagine, we ended up in a couple of places that were not so great. By the end of the trip, we could sleep almost anywhere through almost anything. Here is what we learned.

Where to Sleep

Our favorite place to sleep was on property owned by the Bureau of Land Management (BLM). Not only do they offer free public camping, but they are often in beautiful, tucked-away areas. They are also usually not far from the main interstates. These BLM areas are predominantly found out west. You can find them by searching the web for, "free camping bureau of land management." Many websites can direct you right to them.

There are a couple of downsides to staying at these campgrounds. First of all, sometimes they are hard to find, especially if you are finishing a long day of driving in the dark. To get to the designated pull-off spots, you'll often be led down an unlit gravel road to search for the pull-off spots. They are much easier to find in the daylight.

Second of all, they rarely have running water or facilities. Every once in a while, you will come across a BLM area with some outhouses, but most of the time they are dry campgrounds.

For eleven of the sixty-one nights, we ended up staying in Walmart parking lots. I know it may not be the most attractive option, but before you dismiss the idea, consider the benefits. For starters, they are easy to find in the dark compared to BLM properties. There are also so many of them along main routes. This comes in handy when you get tired and decide to stop driving late at night. There is almost always one soon ahead. They also provide quick access to restrooms and any food you may need to restock before hitting the road. Most of them even have a designated area to RV campers and truckers doing the same thing.

The downside to Walmart is obviously the noise. They are not the most peaceful, quiet place to sleep. Truckers tend to pull in and out late and early, so we liked to try to park far away from them. Every once in a while, you will come upon a Walmart that does not allow overnight parking. You can always ask a manager if you can be an exception. Sometimes they are fine with this since it's often the truckers that they don't want parking overnight.

★ **Relationship Tip:** *Make sure both of you are comfortable with the choice of sleeping location.*

There are other parking lots that sometimes allow overnight parking. For example, we stayed at a Cabelas, Cracker Barrel, a couple of pay-to-park lots, and a few rest-stops. Yet, if these types of parking lots are not clear about if overnight parking is allowed, it's a good idea to ask a manager inside before staying the night. You do not want to be rudely interrupted by a tow truck in the middle of your sleep! For a place such as Cracker Barrel, we thought it polite to ask to stay the night after we had enjoyed eating dinner there. We even went back in the morning to enjoy some hot coffee.

Of course, campgrounds are always another option, and we did pay for a handful of them along the way. They were particularly nice when we wanted a quiet night of sleep. They were also nice for their facilities, showers, and potable water. They also often have fire rings, which was a plus for us.

Wherever you choose to stay, at least do one thing: Park in a level space. It can be a frustrating night if you're sliding into your travel buddy or down to the bottom of your sleeping bag all night long.

Where not to Sleep

Every so often, you may end up stopping to sleep in a place you regret. We had to be diligent about reading the signs in parking lots to figure out if we could stay the night or not. Sometimes it was tempting not to look for any signs or not to read the signs—especially after a long day of driving. We would say, "I didn't read anything saying we couldn't park overnight!" But then one night's misfortune made us a little more careful.

We pulled into a very large parking lot. A casino, an inn, and a couple of other places all shared the lot. We figured with such a big place we could stay unnoticed. Additionally, we knew other vehicles would be around all night long due to the casino and inn.

It was about 2:00 am, and I was fast asleep when all of the sudden there was a "pound, pound, pound!" right on the window by our heads! Christina quickly turned to me, but I was still fast asleep. As the person circled the truck still pounding, she whispered my name and gave me a couple of nudges. I finally woke to this. We remained super quiet, but inside our hearts were racing. I stared at the handle that opens up the cap, knowing that we had no way to lock it from the inside. I kept thinking, "Please don't open it! Please don't open it!" I wondered if the pepper spray was still in the bin between us.

Finally, after what felt like an eternity, the knocking ceased. Christina whispered, "What do we do now!?" "Well, we probably have fifteen minutes before a tow truck comes, if that was a parking inspector," I replied. We agreed we did not want to remain here any longer and we carefully lifted a corner of the curtains to peek outside. We saw no one. So after a few more minutes, we quickly ran around to the front of the truck and pulled away. We found a different parking lot and were finally able to get back to sleep.

We realized we had not been as vigilant as we could have been with picking our spot to sleep. From then on, we paid more attention to signs and places that looked like a bad place to park.

Chapter 14 Takeaways:

- ❑ Bureau of Land Management properties, rest-stops, and campgrounds are all good places to sleep.
- ❑ Multiple websites show locations of BLM lands and other free places to park for the night.
- ❑ Walmart, Cabelas, Cracker Barrel, and pay-to-park parking lots are also easy options.
- ❑ Make sure to ask a store manager if you aren't sure if you are allowed to park overnight.
- ❑ Make sure you read signs and are not parked illegally in order to have a peaceful night.

~ CHAPTER 15 ~

HYGIENE ON THE ROAD

from Melissa's perspective

H aving access to laundromats, showers, and restrooms is very important. These may have crossed your mind when thinking about a big road trip. Some of these may be more important to you than they are to others. But no worries, it is not hard to prioritize any of them. You can spend as much or as little time as you wish pursuing these things.

★ *Relationship Tip: Keep in mind your traveling buddies' preferences when it comes to how often you do laundry and take showers. And try your best to smell decent for each other's sake.*

Laundry

Laundry is fairly easy to do when traveling. Of course, you can stop at laundromats in towns you drive through. Also, many of the bigger national park campground areas offer laundry services. Some of these parks include Shenandoah, Grand Canyon, Crater Lake, Glacier, Yellowstone, and Mammoth Cave. Other campgrounds you stop at may also have laundry services. But do make sure you bring some quarters with you.

The biggest downside for us of doing laundry when traveling was the amount of time it took to stay and wait for the clothes to finish washing and drying! The last time we washed clothes we decided to not even stay and wait for them to dry. Instead, we spread out our clothes in the back of the truck and drove off for an energy-efficient, natural way for them to dry.

Honestly, we had enough clothes packed that we only did laundry a few times on the road. Our little secret to stretching the time between laundry runs was to wash a few essentials in the shower whenever we could. Then we left them on the dash of the truck. On a sunny day they quickly dried right up. It really helped us out!

But, when there is no time for "dash drying," holding wet clothes out the window while the other drives can be a quick alternative to waiting around. I suggest only doing this on a less-busy road. It is a pretty efficient way to dry clothes as long as you do not drop anything in the process. Yet, keep in mind that your buddy may get embarrassed by this.

★ *Relationship Tip: Don't dry clothes out the window if your travel buddy is embarrassed by it. Keep the other's opinions in mind.*

Showers

Similarly to laundromats, you can find showers in multiple national park campgrounds. Again, make sure you have some quarters on hand and be prepared for short, timed showers (usually about five minutes long). Of course, most paid campgrounds or hostels also have showers. Some even allow you to shower for a small price even if you are not staying there—just ask at the check-in office first.

One thing we considered before we left was buying a gym membership to a nation-wide gym with shower facilities. This way we could plan on stopping by to shower whenever going through a city with one of these gyms. But for us, showers were not important enough to redirect our route to stop by gyms. Plus, we felt we wouldn't get our money's worth. Even so, it was a clever idea that might help someone else.

Between national parks and campgrounds, you can find enough opportunities to shower. There are other random places that offer showers that you can find. One time we came across a convenience store in a tiny town that had a shower in the corner of the restroom for a small price. Of course, using body wipes and dry shampoo for those times in-between is a must. Some parks also have bodies of water where you are allowed to swim or wade and even this quick rinse without soap can feel refreshing.

Restrooms

For some, access to restrooms at night may be a concern, but again, it is not too difficult to work around this. Although most free campsites on BLM properties do not have any facilities, there are a few that do and if not, often a gas station is nearby. Walmart parking lots are especially nice for this. Or, you can stick with paying for campgrounds. If you are staying near a national park, often their visitor centers will have at least one restroom with doors unlocked on the outside. Fast-food restaurants and coffee shops often have public restrooms too. Remember that it's always polite to buy something if you are using a restaurant's facilities.

Chapter 15 Takeaways

- ❑ Use laundromat facilities in town, at the parks, or at campgrounds; remember you can wash some items in the shower too.
- ❑ Bring coins for laundromats and showers.
- ❑ Utilize the park's campground showers and bring wipes and dry shampoo for the times in between.
- ❑ Access restrooms outside the visitor centers, at gas stations, restaurants, and Walmart stores; or pay for a campground.

～⌘ CHAPTER 16 ⌘～

IT IS POSSIBLE!

from Christina's perspective

We were very skeptical about the road trip when it was first suggested. Could we really visit forty-seven national parks in one road trip all while living out of a pickup truck? No one had done it before. So how would someone like us be able to do it? We couldn't extinguish the burning desire to give it a try and do something crazy! The idea excited us, and we had to see if it was possible.

We were blazing the trail. We were doing something that had never been done. We pulled out of the driveway in the truck with high hopes, real fears, and so much uncertainty. We were still unsure of how the trip would come together. But we were excited to be living a new, crazy, different lifestyle of adventure on the road.

We knew that branching out on our own would be a good experience for both of us. Having always lived at home, we thought that the time on the road would be great for personal growth. We knew we would miss our friends and family and the comforts of home, but it would be good for us to live and learn on our own.

We knew we would get homesick and lonely, but we were excited for the opportunity. We knew that everyone was just a phone call away and that we would only be away for two months. Both of us were especially excited for the opportunity to see God's creation. We believed that a trip like this would be healthy for our relationships with Him.

After traveling a grand total of 18,684 miles, our home on wheels was back on home soil! We are so thankful that we took The Ultimate Road Trip. We had the time of our lives and we made memories that will last a lifetime! We experienced personal growth and we grew even closer to each other. We also grew closer to our Creator—the Creator of the universe. His handiwork is something else! Get out there and see it. You won't regret it!

After pushing ourselves to do this crazy road trip we were more confident and open to new opportunities. We both returned with eagerness to dream, more confidence in our own abilities, and a new awareness of the world around us.

If we had decided not to do the road trip, we would still be wondering if we could have done it. We would be looking at other people's photos and thinking, "that could have been us." But that was us! And we have no regrets! Yes, we were hesitant, scared and unsure at first. But we knew that whether or not we saw all of the parks, beautiful things would come of the trip. The road trip left us with countless memories of some of the best days of our lives. It was worth far beyond the price tag that came with it.

This could be you too! We know that it is possible to drive to all of the mainland United States national parks all within two months. And we know that you can do it too. If traveling is something that you've dreamed about for a while, maybe it's on your heart for a reason. At least give yourself the opportunity. No matter what your hopes and dreams are, I want to encourage you to be intentional with your life. You only get one! There will always be hesitation and fear to do something new. But what would your life look like without "fear." Would you do something that your usual self would think is crazy?

We hope that this book alleviates your fears and leaves you with all the information you need to go take your own ultimate road trip!

APPENDIX

Step by step instructions and measurements for our platform build for a 2006 Chevy Colorado™ truck

First of all, you need to determine the height of the platform. From the top of the truck cap to the plywood floor we would have in the truck bed we had 38 inches. We went with making the platform 12 inches above the wooden floor in the bed of the truck. This left us with plenty of storage and yet adequate head space. After determining the height, we cut the dividing boards. With the platform being at 12 inches from the wooden floor, the platform would sit above the wheel wells, giving us a large, flat surface area to sleep on.

Step 1

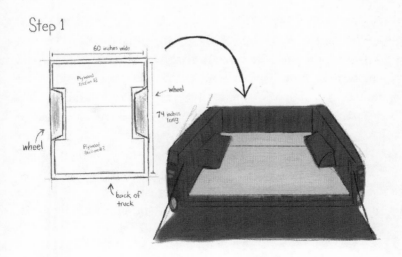

<u>Step 1 - Build a floor</u>: We first cut some of the plywood to fit the floor of the truck bed. This gave us a level floor and something we could fasten things into. We left a few inches at the tailgate end of the floor just to be sure that the tailgate would be able to hinge open freely.

Step 2

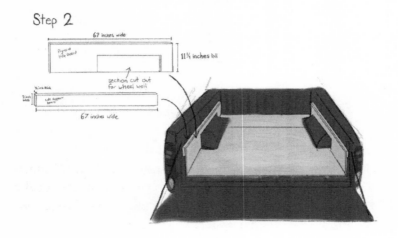

<u>Step 2 - Cutting the two wheel well support boards</u>: With ¾ inch plywood, cut two support boards that will go over the wheel wells and run the length of the truck bed. These two boards are 11 ¼ inches by 67 inches. These two boards had a large section cut out to fit over the wheel well but still close to the side of the truck. On the side of the wheel well support board that was against the side of the truck add a ¾ inch thick, 3 inch by 67 inch piece of wood. This strengthened the support board that had such a large section cut out to go over the wheel well. It also keeps the wheel well support board from starting to split when screwing into it.

Step 3

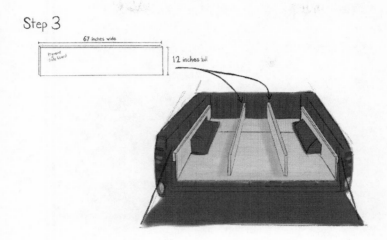

Step 3 - Cutting the two center support boards: With ¾ inch plywood, cut two support boards that go down the center of the truck bed and that run the length of the truck bed. These two boards were 12 inches wide and 67 inches long.

*****Notice***** The sides of the truck bed angle slightly outward. In other words, the bottom of the truck bed is slightly narrower than 12 inches above the bottom of the truck bed where the platform will be. For that reason, we planned to have the platform boards that were up against the sides of the truck hang over the wheel well support boards. The two wheel well support boards were cut ¾ inch shorter than the two center support boards. This allowed the platform to rest on the wheel well support boards and to extend over the wheel well support board. Allowing the platform to be flush against the side of the truck.

Step 4

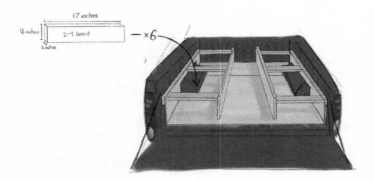

<u>Step 4 - Building the "bed frame"</u>: Using three 17-inch-long 2x4s, we fastened the two right hand side support boards to each other. Creating a free standing "bed frame." Again, using three 17 inch long 2x4s we fastened the two left hand side support boards together.

Step 5

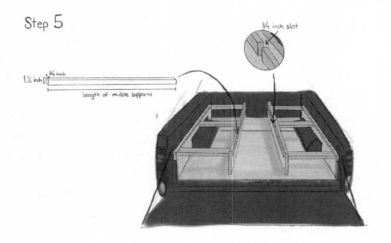

Step 5 - Adding a lip: Add a lip on both sides of the two center support boards. This gives the platform boards a place to rest. The lip sits ¾ inch down from the surface of the platform. Allowing the platform to sit on the lip. The lip is a ¾ inch thick piece of plywood that is 1 ½ inch wide. Leave a ¾ gap with no lip. This left a ¾ inch slot where a board on the bottom of a platform board could fit in. (See Step 8)

*****Notice*****There was no need to add a lip on the wheel well support boards, seeing as the platform will rest on top of the wheel well support boards.

Step 6

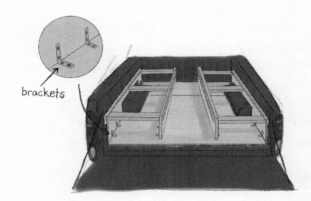

brackets

Step 6 - Fastening the "bed frame" to the floor: Before cutting the plywood boards for the platform, screw the "bed frame" to the floor using brackets. Using brackets instead of a strip of wood gives more space for storage bins. It also makes it easier to take the platform out of the truck and to reassemble it again later.

Step 7

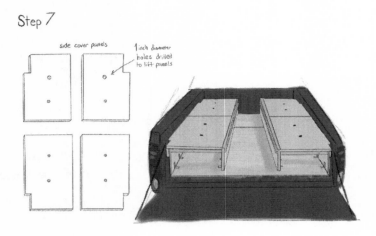

<u>Step 7 - Cut the platform boards</u>: The next step was to cut the boards for the platform. We chose to have 6 separate pieces of platform to allow easy access to storage below. In a sense, creating 6 storage compartments. The two sections that made up the middle of the platform were perfect rectangles. The four on the outside edges of the truck bed were rectangular with a few notches cut out of it to fit flush against the sides of the truck bed. We made the platform 2 inches short of the tailgate. This allowed for our sleeping bags to hang over the platform and not get smashed in by the tailgate.

Also drill holes in the platform boards. This makes it so that you can easily pick up the platform panels from inside the truck bed. The holes are 1 inch in diameter, and they divide each section of the platform into thirds.

Step 8

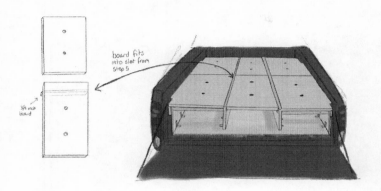

board fits
into slot from
step 5

3/4 inch
board

Step 8 - Add more lip: In order to keep the sections of the platform from sliding around add a lip on the bottom of the platforms that fit right into the ¾ inch space that was left in step 5.

The final surface of the platform is 60in by 72in.

Recipes for on the Road

BREAKFASTS

Muffin Mix Pancakes

Time: About ten minutes from start to finish
Cooking Tools Required:
- Camp stove with propane and a lighter
- Skillet
- Flipper spatula
- Measuring cup
- Fork
- Spoon

Ingredients:
- Oil
- "Just add water or milk" muffin mix package
- Water
- Powdered milk (optional)

Directions:
1) Light your stove and place your skillet on the burner over medium heat.
2) Add oil to lightly cover the bottom of the skillet.
3) Tear open the muffin mix bag along the top and pour in the amount of water listed on the package (usually about half of a cup).
4) Add a couple spoonfuls of powdered milk if desired.
5) Use the fork to mix up the batter within the package until well mixed. Batter should be thick, but easy to pour out. Add more water if necessary.
6) Squeeze the batter into the skillet into four pancakes and let cook for about five minutes or until the middle of the pancake starts to bubble. If using a small skillet, you may need to do two pancakes at a time.

7) Flip pancakes and let cook for two to three more minutes.

8) Remove from heat and enjoy.

Serves two hungry hikers.

Pancakes

Time: About fifteen minutes from start to finish

Cooking Tools Required:
- Camp stove with propane and a lighter
- Skillet
- Flipper spatula
- Measuring cup
- Blender bottle with whisk

Ingredients:
- Oil
- "Just add water" pancake mix
- Water

Directions:
1) Light your stove and place your skillet on the burner over medium heat.

2) Add oil to lightly cover the bottom of the skillet.

3) Use the directions on the box to determine the water-to-mix ratio. Usually one cup of mix with three-fourths cup of water makes enough pancakes for two adults.

4) Add the pancake mix and water to the blender bottle and shake well.

5) Pour mixture into the pan in making three or four pancakes at a time.

6) Cook for a few minutes until pancakes start to bubble in the middle. Flip and cook for a couple more minutes.

7) Remove from heat and repeat with remaining batter starting with adding oil.

8) Top with apple pancake topping and enjoy! (See next recipe.)

Serves two hungry hikers.

Apple Pancake Topping

Time: About twenty minutes from start to finish

Cooking Tools Required:
- Camp stove with propane and a lighter
- Saucepan with lid
- Sharp knife
- Cutting board
- Heat-resistant spoon
- Measuring spoons

Ingredients:
- Apples
- Butter
- Brown sugar
- Cinnamon

Directions:
1) Cut up one large or two small apples into thin slices.
2) Light your stove and place your saucepan on the burner over medium-low heat.
3) Melt about one tablespoon of butter in the saucepan.
4) Add the apple slices.
5) Stir in two tablespoons of brown sugar and about ¼ teaspoon of cinnamon.
6) Place the lid on the saucepan and let the apples cook for about fifteen minutes while stirring occasionally.
7) When apples are soft and the mixture has thickened, remove from heat and place on top of pancakes.

Serves two hungry hikers.

DINNERS

Pasta Entrees

Time: About thirty minutes from start to finish
Cooking Tools Required:
- Camp stove with propane and a lighter
- Saucepan with lid
- Heat-resistant spoon
- Can opener
- Measuring cup

Ingredients:
- Water
- Powdered milk
- Pasta mix
- Butter (optional)
- Can of vegetables of choice
- Can of pre-cooked chicken

Directions:
1) Light your stove and place your saucepan on the burner over medium heat.
2) Add water to the saucepan. Use the directions on the pasta package to determine how much.
3) If the package calls for milk, add enough water in place of the milk and add about two spoonfuls of powdered milk.
4) Add about a tablespoon of butter.
5) Place the lid on the pan and let the liquids boil before adding the package contents.
6) Cook the pasta uncovered for about seven minutes while stirring occasionally.
7) As the mixture cooks, open and drain the can of vegetables and the chicken.
8) Add the vegetables and chicken into the mixture as it finishes cooking.

9) Reduce heat, place the lid back on the saucepan, and let the mixture sit for a couple of minutes for sauce to thicken. Enjoy!

Serves two hungry hikers.

Ramen Bombs

Time: About thirty minutes from start to finish
Cooking Tools Required:
- Camp stove with propane and a lighter
- Saucepan with lid
- Heat-resistant spoon
- Measuring cup

Ingredients:
- Water
- Ramen noodles
- Instant mashed potatoes

Directions:
1) Light your stove and place your saucepan on the burner.
2) Cook the ramen noodles according to the package instructions.
3) Once ramen noodles are almost finished cooking, add enough instant potatoes to thicken the mixture.
4) If the mixture gets too thick, add more water.
5) Once smooth and warm remove from heat and enjoy.

Serves two hungry hikers.

Tacos

Time: About twenty minutes from start to finish
Cooking Tools Required:
- Camp stove with propane and a lighter
- Skillet
- Saucepan
- Heat-resistant spoons
- Spatula
- Can opener

Ingredients:
- Canned chicken
- Can of baked beans
- Rice package
- Water
- Tortillas

Directions:
1) Light your stove.
2) Cook the rice in the saucepan according to directions.
3) As the rice is cooking, warm up the can of chicken in one half of the skillet and the baked beans in the other half.
4) Once all ingredients are cooked and warmed through, spread on a tortilla and enjoy.

(Note: if you are near a grocery store you can buy and add salsa, cheese, and sour cream)
Serves two hungry hikers.

DESSERTS

Peach Cobbler

Time: About twenty minutes from start to finish

Cooking Tools Required:
- Camp stove with propane and a lighter
- Saucepan with lid
- Mixing bowl
- Heat-resistant serving spoon
- Fork
- Can opener

Extra Necessity:
- Grocery or convenience store nearby

Ingredients:
- 1 can of peaches in syrup
- Pancake mix
- Oats
- Brown sugar
- Cinnamon
- Butter

Directions:
1) Place the peaches with syrup into the saucepan and whisk in a few spoonfuls of pancake mix.
2) Light the stove and place a lid on the pan. Let the mixture warm and thicken over medium-low heat. Stir occasionally.
3) While that's warming up, mix in a separate bowl the following: a couple of handfuls of oats, a spoonful of brown sugar, a sprinkle of cinnamon, and a couple tablespoons of butter.
4) When the peaches are hot and bubbly, sprinkle this crumble mixture over the peaches.

5) Place the lid back on the pot and move the pot from the fast cooking burner to the slow cooking burner (or reduce heat if that's an option for you).
6) Let simmer on the low burner for about five minutes.
7) While it's simmering, send your travel buddy inside the grocery store to buy vanilla ice cream to enjoy with the cobbler.

Serves two hungry hikers.

Caramel Popcorn

Time: About ten minutes from start to finish
Cooking Tools Required:
- Camp stove with propane and a lighter
- Saucepan with lid
- Dish towel or two hot pads
- Heat-resistant spoon
- Medium dish tub or large bowl
- Measuring cup

Ingredients:
- Popcorn kernels
- Oil
- Butter
- Brown sugar
- Honey
- Baking soda

Directions:
1) Pour enough oil into a saucepan to lightly coat the bottom of the pan.
2) Light the stove and turn the burner up to as hot as it goes.
3) With the saucepan on the burner, place a couple of handfuls of popcorn kernels into the pot.
4) Place the lid on the saucepan and use a dishtowel to grab the pan and gently shake as the popcorn pops.

5) Once popped, transfer the popcorn into the tub or bowl.

6) Wipe out the saucepan and add about four tablespoons of butter, half a cup of brown sugar, and three table-spoons of honey.

7) Stir often as the mixture warms up.

8) Right before it boils, remove from heat and add to the mixture about three-fourths of a teaspoon of baking soda and quickly stir. The mixture will become foamy.

9) Pour the warm mixture into the tub of popcorn and stir well before enjoying.

Serves two hungry hikers.

Cookies

Time: About fifteen minutes from start to finish.
Cooking Tools Required:
- Camp stove with propane and a lighter
- Skillet
- Flipping spatula
- Fork
- Measuring spoon

Ingredients:
- Oil
- Package of instant cookie mix

Directions:
1) Light your stove and place your skillet on the burner.

2) Add enough oil to lightly coat the bottom of the skillet.

3) While the oil is warming up, cut open the top of the cookie mix package. Add the oil per package instructions and use the fork to stir well.

4) Pour the mixture into the skillet as one big pancake.

5) Once the cookie starts to thicken and bubble, flip it best you can. (It will likely fall apart).

6) Continue to stir and flip until cooked.

7) Remove from heat and enjoy. (Best eaten in a bowl with a fork.)

Serves two hungry hikers.

Traveler's Smores

Time: About fifteen minutes from start to finish (or cook while hiking).

Required:
- A sunny day
- Your vehicle

Ingredients:
- Bag of marshmallows
- Chocolate bars
- Graham crackers

Directions:
1) On a sunny day, leave the marshmallows on the dash while you are off hiking or set the bag on the hot roof of the vehicle if you are staying around the parking lot.
2) Let the bag rest until the marshmallows are melted.
3) If you like your chocolate also melted, place a graham cracker and a piece of chocolate on the hot roof or inside the hood of your vehicle.
4) Once marshmallows are gooey, cut a corner of the bag and squeeze out enough marshmallow to generously cover a graham cracker.
5) Place chocolate and another graham cracker on top and enjoy.

Master Packing List

Clothing:
- ☐ Rain jacket
- ☐ 2 hoodies
- ☐ 10 t-shirts or tanks
- ☐ Water resistant pants
- ☐ Warm leggings
- ☐ 7 pairs of shorts
- ☐ 5 pairs of pants
- ☐ 14 pairs of socks
- ☐ Lots of underwear
- ☐ Hiking shoes
- ☐ Athletic shoes
- ☐ Flip flops or sandals
- ☐ Belt
- ☐ Hat
- ☐ Swimsuit
- ☐ Winter hat and gloves
- ☐ Sunglasses

Miscellaneous:
- ☐ 2 towels
- ☐ 2 washcloths
- ☐ Laundry soap
- ☐ Bug spray
- ☐ Sunscreen
- ☐ Aloe
- ☐ Vitamins or supplements
- ☐ Pocketknife
- ☐ Cloth or drawstring bag

Hygiene:
- ❑ Toiletry bag
- ❑ Toothbrush and toothpaste
- ❑ Hairbrush and hair accessories
- ❑ Shampoo and conditioner
- ❑ Bar of soap or body wash
- ❑ Razor
- ❑ Hand sanitizer
- ❑ Body wipes
- ❑ Deodorant
- ❑ Lip balm
- ❑ Lotion
- ❑ Nail clippers
- ❑ Tissues

Camping equipment:
- ❑ Warm sleeping bag
- ❑ Large sleeping bag (to put the foam mat inside)
- ❑ Foam camping mat(s) (double them up if you like more cushion)
- ❑ Hammock with a bug net
- ❑ Pillow
- ❑ Extra blanket
- ❑ Headlight
- ❑ Day pack with a water bladder
- ❑ Water bottle
- ❑ Fire starter

Safety and precaution items:
- ❑ Lockable safe
- ❑ Gun
- ❑ Pepper spray
- ❑ Spare keys
- ❑ First aid kit

- ❑ Ibuprofen
- ❑ Band-Aids of various sizes
- ❑ Neosporin
- ❑ Gauze
- ❑ Jumper cables
- ❑ Toolbox

Travel items:
- ❑ Passport
- ❑ Wallet
- ❑ National park pass
- ❑ Envelope with cash
- ❑ Daily itinerary
- ❑ Any ferry or tour tickets
- ❑ Paper maps (at least one large map of the U.S.)

Technology and entertainment:
- ❑ Laptops and charging cords
- ❑ Extension cord with a power strip
- ❑ Power inverter (see chapter 9)
- ❑ Camera/ GoPro™/ and batteries or chargers
- ❑ USB phone charger
- ❑ Phone mount
- ❑ Headphones
- ❑ A couple of books
- ❑ Index cards (see chapter 12)

Kitchen items:
- ❑ Camping stove
- ❑ Propane
- ❑ Lighter
- ❑ One small-sized pot
- ❑ One medium-sized pot with a lid
- ❑ One medium-sized skillet

- ❑ Thin plastic cutting board
- ❑ Blender bottle with whisk
- ❑ Can opener
- ❑ Heat resistant serving spoon
- ❑ Rubber spatula
- ❑ Flipper spatula
- ❑ Whisk
- ❑ Pair of tongs
- ❑ Scissors
- ❑ Paring knife
- ❑ Set of measuring cups and spoons
- ❑ Two hot pads
- ❑ Small collapsible cooler
- ❑ 4 sporks
- ❑ 3 plates
- ❑ 4 plastic bowls
- ❑ Extra set of plastic silverware
- ❑ Collapsible roasting sticks
- ❑ Coffee thermoses
- ❑ Plastic pour over coffee drippers
- ❑ Coffee filters
- ❑ Dish drying towels
- ❑ Dish soap
- ❑ Scrub brush/scraper
- ❑ Foil
- ❑ Sandwich bags
- ❑ A few plastic grocery bags
- ❑ 2 large storage bins with lids
- ❑ 2 large open bins
- ❑ 1 medium dish pan
- ❑ 2 shoe box size bins with lids
- ❑ Storage cube bin
- ❑ Non-skid grip shelf liner
- ❑ Travel size broom with dustpan

Food Basics:
- ❑ A few favorite seasonings
- ❑ Brown sugar
- ❑ Butter
- ❑ Canola oil
- ❑ Cinnamon
- ❑ Honey
- ❑ Maple syrup
- ❑ One gallon of water
- ❑ Parmesan cheese
- ❑ Popcorn salt
- ❑ Powdered milk
- ❑ Salt and pepper

Breakfasts:
- ❑ Granola/ or another cereal
- ❑ Individual boxes of milk (that don't require refrigeration)
- ❑ Grits or cream of wheat
- ❑ Ground coffee
- ❑ Muffin mix (just add water type)
- ❑ Oatmeal
- ❑ Pancake mix (just add water)

Lunches and Snacks:
- ❑ Applesauce packages
- ❑ Beef jerky
- ❑ Canned chicken or tuna
- ❑ Canned fruit
- ❑ Dried fruit
- ❑ Fresh fruit (like bananas, apples, cherries, grapes)
- ❑ Fresh veggies (like carrots and snap peas)
- ❑ Granola bars
- ❑ Jelly
- ❑ Mayo packets

- ❏ Peanut butter
- ❏ Popcorn kernels
- ❏ Salty snacks (like pretzels, or crackers)
- ❏ Tortilla wraps or a loaf of bread
- ❏ Trail mixes

Dinners:
- ❏ Canned soup
- ❏ Canned veggies
- ❏ Fresh veggies
- ❏ Instant mashed potatoes
- ❏ Ramen noodles
- ❏ Rice
- ❏ Baked beans for tacos (using the tortillas and canned chicken from lunch)
- ❏ Variety of quick stovetop meals
- ❏ Stir fry ingredients

Sweet Treats:
- ❏ Chocolate chip cookie mix (We used the Betty Crocker™ brand.)
- ❏ Instant pudding box
- ❏ Can of peaches
- ❏ Baking soda
- ❏ Marshmallows
- ❏ Graham crackers
- ❏ Chocolate bars

We hope you have enjoyed this book.

If this book has helped you embark on a road trip, we would love to hear from you and see pictures. Or if you have any questions or comments, send us an email at theultimateroadtripguide@gmail.com

Made in the USA
Coppell, TX
12 June 2022